Heroes Publishing

AFTER THE VILLA

life without the lions

by
Dave Woodhall

First published in Great Britain in 2005 by
Heroes Publishing.
P.O. Box, Perry Barr,
Birmingham B42 1UZ.
www.heroespublishing.com

The rights of Dave Woodhall to be identified as author of this work has been asserted by him in accordance with the Copyright, Design and Patents Act 1988.

All rights reserved. No part of this publication may be reproduced, stored in a retrieval system or transmitted in any form or by any means electronic, digital, mechanical, recording or otherwise without the prior permission of the publisher.

ISBN 0-9543884-3-7

Printed by Antony Rowe, Chippenham

Acknowledgements

For much of this page, I may as well have just put 'same as last time.' Neil Rioch of the Aston Villa Former Players Association continues to amaze me with the amount of information he was able to obtain regarding his ex-comrades scattered around the globe. Andy Wainwright and Peter Page once more proof-read until their eyes were falling out, while Greg Upton forever pointed out statistical errors. And of course, the Divine Ms J pushed me out into enough cold, grey dawns to make sure that I finished the thing on time.

Then there were the players themselves. I travelled far and wide, by plane, train and automobile to meet former footballers in a variety of circumstances. At cricket grounds, football grounds, training grounds, hotels, in the backs of taxis, and in the odd licensed premise. Many were kind enough to let me into their homes; all provided a mine of information, far more than I would ever have been able to obtain by myself. And every one disproved that old adage about how you should never meet your heroes, because they'll only let you down. During the writing of this book, I met many of my heroes, and every one of them proved worthy of the title. I've always believed that the greatest honour that can be bestowed upon anyone is to play for Aston Villa, and the men I spoke to have all proved themselves in every way worthy of such distinction. Thank you, one and all.

Thanks also to Tony Scholes, Keith Whitmore, Ken Grime, Richard Whitehead, Andy Mitten, Mac McColgan, Martin Morris, Pat Murphy, Martin Swain, Andy Poole, Dave Collett, Geoff Allman, Ash Connor and Tony Scholes for the assistance they gave to the project.

Finally, it was during the writing of this book that everyone connected with the Villa was saddened to learn of the death of Terry Weir. Terry captured Villa Park history as it was taking place in such a unique and gifted way that he became part of the club's folklore, and he certainly helped me in more ways than he could have imagined. I would therefore like to dedicate this work to Terence Francis Weir; Villa photographer for many years and Villa supporter for a lifetime.

Contents

List of Illustrations   9
Introduction   11

IN GOAL

Jim Cumbes   15

AT THE BACK

George Curtis   27
John Gidman   33
Dennis Jackson   41
Ivor Linton   47
Ian Ross   53
Shaun Teale   61

IN THE MIDDLE

Paul Birch   75
Jimmy Brown   83
Alex Cropley   89
Alan Deakin   97
Ian Hamilton   103
Kevin Richardson   109
Mike Tindall   117

OUT WIDE

Harry Burrows   125
Stephen Froggatt   131
Ray Graydon   143
Peter McParland   153
Ian Ormondroyd   161
Mark Walters   171

UP FRONT

Tony Cascarino   183
Graham Fenton   195
Tony Hateley   203
Keith Leonard   209
Andy Lochhead   215
Sammy Morgan   223

List of Illustrations

Cover:	**Trinity Road, Aston – October 2005**
	Photo: Heroes Publishing
Plate 1:	**Ray Graydon after Walsall's victory in the Division Two Play-Off final – May 2001**
	Photo: Express & Star
Plate 2:	**Wolverhampton Wanderers – 1962/63**
	Photo: Express & Star
Plate 3:	**West Bromwich Albion – 1971/72**
	Photo: Express & Star
Plate 4:	**Ian Ormondroyd – Oldham v WBA – 1997**
	Photo: Express & Star
Plate 5:	**Paul Birch – Wolves v Stoke City – 1993**
	Photo: Express & Star
Plate 6:	**Paul Birch and Steve Bull – November 1993**
	Photo: Express & Star
Plate 7:	**Kevin Richardson being sent off for Coventry at Villa Park – December 1995**
	Photo: Express & Star
Plate 8:	**Stephen Froggatt – Wolves v Sunderland**
	Photo: Express & Star
Plate 9:	**Graham Fenton – August 1995**
	Photo: Express & Star
Plate 10:	**Shaun Teale – August 1995**
	Photo: Express & Star
Plate 11:	**Sammy Morgan in a presentation at Norwich City**
	Photo: Keith Whitmore
Plate 12:	**John Gidman – Manchester United v West Bromwich Albion – February 1985**
	Photo: Express & Star
Plate 13:	**Andy Lochhead at Burnley**
	Photo: Tony Scholes

Introduction

If I began by saying nostalgia ain't what it used to be, you'd be within your rights to put this book back on the shelf and walk away. Cliches should be avoided like the plague and anyway, nostalgia is bigger and better now than ever before. It seems that every walk of life is being Reunited, so it's only fair that the former players of that unique and unpredictable institution known as the Aston Villa Football Club should be accorded the same treatment.

When I decided to track down and talk to Villa players of the past, find out what they were doing now and learn how they'd got there, I laid down a few ground rules. First, no current players; I didn't really want to talk to anyone who was still playing professionally. I also didn't want to feature the stars of the eighties who had won the league and European Cup. For one thing, you can read all about them in my previous book Champions (available from all good bookshops, ISBN 0-9543884-2-9 if there's a problem). And for another, I'd harassed them all so much during its writing that if I were to contact them again, restraining orders would likely have been the result.

There wasn't much point, either, in highlighting those former players who had left the Villa and, difficult though it is to believe that such a possibility exists, found even greater fame and fortune elsewhere. When they're on television every week, it doesn't take a genius to find out what they're doing with themselves.

The type of ex-players I wanted to speak to were men who had unusual careers after their footballing days ended, and I certainly found those. Amongst others there's a missionary, a professional gambler, a couple of youth workers, a fireman-in-waiting and the man in charge of one of the biggest clubs in British sport. They're the sort of people who, whenever their name is mentioned, invariably provoke the response, "I wonder what he's doing now?" In 26 cases, here's the answer.

IN GOAL

Jim Cumbes

Old Trafford is, without doubt, one of the great sporting venues of the world. Even during the close-season, when there's no-one around except the groundstaff, it maintains an atmosphere that exudes memories of never to be forgotten occasions and wonderful performances by legends of the game. Sitting in the office of the club's chief executive, it's difficult to imagine he is able to get much work done, enjoying as he does a view that extends over luxurious turf which, even weeks away from the start of a new season, remains a hive of activity.

But it's a distraction which Jim Cumbes, chief executive of Lancashire County Cricket Club, based at the original Old Trafford a few hundred yards from the football ground which stole its name in 1908, can live with. "It's not the best view in the world," he says, disarmingly. "The chief executive at Lords has his office behind the bowler's arm." Neither does it prevent Cumbes from being an interviewer's dream. Twice I've spoken to him, twice I've left his office with ribs sore from laughter, close to three hours after my arrival. Talking to Jim Cumbes may be many things: An education certainly, an eye-opener without a doubt, but it's far too enjoyable to count as proper work.

Jim was, of course, one of the last of that band of multi-talented sportsmen who played first-class cricket during the summer months and league football the rest of the year. They've all gone now, victims of both the ever-extending football season and of the need for greater dedication in either discipline. And another unique feature of British sporting life has sadly passed with them.

Jim was born in Didsbury, Manchester, in 1944. Leaving school at the age of seventeen, he worked for a time for an insurance company before being offered a trial with Lancashire in 1962. This led to the offer of a season-long contract, which was quickly extended to three years, and left the young fast bowler in somewhat of a dilemma. "In those days, cricketers were only on a six-month contract, to cover the season. So, because I'd had to give my job up to play for Lancs, there was the problem of how to earn a living during the winter. I worked as a packer, a driver, I sold key insurance – I bet you've never met anyone who's done that before."

However, fate was to not only lend a hand in providing Cumbes with a winter income, it was also to make him a member of what was already a dying breed of versatile sportsmen. "I'd played football at school, but packed up the game when I started work. Then I was taking part in a charity match, and on the strength of how well I did there I was offered a contract with Runcorn Town, who were in the Cheshire League. I was going to be in the reserve side; it was 30 shillings a week out of the cricket season, which was fine by me. I played in the first team, we got to the Cheshire Cup final against Tranmere, and we won after a replay. This would have been in 1965. Tranmere had a few injuries, they had no cover for their keepers, and so they signed me on the back of that display in the final. Right place, right time.

"Four years later I'd become a first team regular and we were playing Port Vale in the League Cup. I had a good game and I didn't know it then, but a scout was watching the game and recommended me to the Albion manager, Alan Ashman, who was looking for cover for John Osborne. Right place, right time again, and once more I was going to be an understudy."

Cumbes had made 137 appearances for Tranmere, and a fee of £8,000 took him to the Hawthorns. Albion at the time were one of the best sides in the country, and on their way to the 1969-70 League Cup final. Cumbes, however, would be unable to join them at Wembley. "I was cup-tied because of that match against Port Vale, which meant that John Osborne was always getting picked for the league games ahead of me because, as the cup run progressed, he offered more continuity in the side."

Cumbes spent almost three seasons at the Hawthorns, playing 64 first team games, before Vic Crowe decided that he was the man to fill what had long been a problem position at Villa. The keeper himself was equally sure of the move, not least because, for once in his career, he would be first-choice goalkeeper. "I didn't get on with

Don Howe, who had become the Albion manager by then. I thought I'd been playing well but he'd still drop me, saying that the team couldn't afford errors. Vic came in and the fact that Villa were getting bigger crowds than the Albion despite being two divisions lower was a big factor in my decision. Everyone knew they were going places. I told Don I was off, and he tried to persuade me to stay at Albion, but the two of us would never have got on."

Jim moved to Villa Park for £35,000, making his debut in a 6-0 win away at Oldham. He stayed with the club throughout the run that took in the third division title and then promotion from the second division, with the 1975 League Cup final win at Wembley as a bonus.

It would be fair to say that the outgoing Cumbes, who moonlighted as a presenter on BBC Radio Birmingham during his time with Villa, would never see eye to eye with the plain-speaking, totally professional, Ron Saunders. The manager was astute enough to realise that the squad he inherited from Vic Crowe in the summer of 1974 needed little reinforcing to win promotion, and so it proved. However, staying in the first division required major team-rebuilding and Cumbes was one of the casualties, losing his place in the side following the 5-1 aggregate defeat to Antwerp in the UEFA Cup and never again playing for the first team. He had made a total of 181 appearances, taking his total in professional football to almost 400 - quite a feat for a player who had begun his career as a stand-in with Runcorn Town reserves.

Granted a free transfer at the end of the 1975-76 season, Cumbes was one of the many players to head across the Atlantic, joining the sizeable Villa connection at Portland Timbers over on the Pacific coast. "Vic was manager, the late Brian Tiler was his coach, Pat McMahon was there, as was Neil Rioch, and Peter Withe had played for them the summer before. I loved the States, and they certainly showed us how to market the game. We also did a lot of coaching while we were over there. The kids were really enthusiastic about football, but they were so naïve. We'd roll a ball to them along the floor, and whereas a kid over here would be able to kick even when they were four or five, roll the ball even to a thirteen year old American and they'd swing and miss. We couldn't work out why they were so bad at football until one day we were on the coach and we were watching some lads with a ball up against a wall. Over here they'd have been kicking the ball, but these were throwing it and that's when I realised – every game kids played in America involved them using their hands."

In fact, so ingrained into the American sports psyche is the avoidance of feet wherever possible, that Jim found himself in demand as a specialist kicker in American Football. "They called me 'Bigfoot' over there, because of the length I could kick a football, and the colleges asked me to be a specialist field kicker. I thought about it but decided to turn them down. It's a much heavier ball even than our rugby ball, and it wasn't easy."

Cumbes stayed just one summer in Portland, despite a personality that seemed tailor-made for the United States. "Vic asked me to play there the following summer, and if I'd have been younger I would have gone back, but I enjoyed playing cricket too much. I reckoned I'd got five or six years left in cricket, but I wouldn't have had that much time playing football. I explained the situation to Vic, and he understood. He said 'Most of the players who stay here haven't got anything to go back for, but you have'."

Returning to England at the beginning of the 1976-77 season, Cumbes began an odyssey that could best be described as 'Rent-a-Keeper.' He explains, "Ron Wylie was at Coventry and he asked me to help him out there because their reserve keeper, Bryan King, was out for a time and they only had Jim Blyth available. I stayed until virtually the end of the season, but although Jim had a few knocks he was always fit when matchday came round. Then in what was almost the last game he was finally ruled out, but by then I was back playing cricket and a young lad named Les Sealey made his debut."

By now Cumbes, together with his one-time rival for the Albion keeper's jersey and later firm friend and business colleague, John Osborne, were recognised fixtures in many a local manager's contacts book.

"Ossie and I started a sports retail business in 1973. We bought the former Wolves goalie Bert Williams' shop in Bilston, which is where I met my wife, and we opened a market stall as well. Both of us would also turn out for any club that needed a keeper in an emergency. In fact, Ossie suggested starting up a service called Goalkeeping Samaritans. I played for Runcorn again, played a few games for Stourbridge in the Southern League, and made ten appearances for Southport before they went out of the league.

"Then Nobby Clarke, who was the manager of Worcester City, asked me to step in for them when their keeper broke his wrist. It should have been for six games but, Nobby being the character he was, I ended up there for four years. We won the Southern Premier League, and there were over 8,000 at the ground on the night we made sure of the title by beating Kettering. There was great potential at Worcester. It was always said that they had more going for them then than Kidderminster did when they got into the league, but Worcester had the problem that they could never expand the ground because it's surrounded by housing all round.

"Nobby was a brilliant manager at that level. He never wanted to manage in the Football League; he knew the non-league scene and that was where he was happiest. His pre-match talks were typical Nobby. The trainer would give us the usual stuff about the opposition and how we'd be playing, then at the end Nobby would chip in with 'And don't forget the win bonus'.

"I played for Worcester until 1982, when my daughter was born. I told Nobby that he'd asked me to play six games and I'd played 104, so it was about time I hung my boots up and, apart from a few charity games, I've never played football since then."

Jim may have given up football, but he was still far from an ex-sportsman. After two seasons with Surrey and a brief return to Lancashire, he had moved to Worcestershire in 1972, linking up at the picturesque New Road ground with two more league footballers: Phil Neale, who played over 350 times for Lincoln City, and Sheffield United's Ted Hemsley, himself a veteran of almost 300 games. The highlight of Cumbes' cricketing career occurred in 1974 when Worcestershire won the county championship, but by 1981 they had decided that his time at New Road should end. "Warwickshire offered me a contract for the 1982 season as cover for Bob Willis, who was away with England a lot of the time, and also asked me to coach the second XI. I played a few games in the first team, which I didn't expect."

It was at this time that Cumbes, ironically, in view of a long career as a top-flight goalkeeper, suffered what was to be the worst injury of his sporting career. "I was playing at Leicester in a Sunday

League game when I dived for the ball and fell awkwardly – it had to be a one-day competition, I wouldn't have dived in a county championship match. I felt as though I'd got a rope drawing around my chest, I couldn't get my breath and in the end I had to leave the field and go to hospital. With it being a Sunday the hospital was pretty quiet, but I thought I was having a heart attack, so they wired me up to an ECG machine and did all the tests. That showed nothing. I went home for the night and drove to hospital in Birmingham the following day. I had x-rays and it took an hour before they found out that I had a collapsed lung. When the doctor found I'd driven from Leicester the night before, she had a fit and said I could have sued the hospital 'for everything they've got'. In the end I was detained in hospital for ten days."

Cumbes made a full return to fitness and made several more appearances for Warwickshire. By now, though, his career was moving in a different direction and one in which such an outgoing personality was perfectly suited, although it had taken him a few years to realise the fact. "Round about 1979, Bill Bothwell, who was Tranmere's chairman, asked me if I'd be interested in becoming their commercial manager. I was flattered, but I knew that it would be a tough job and I still wanted to play cricket at the time. I was approached to be assistant to Les Thornley at Albion, then, in 1980, Worcestershire asked me to do the job, but that fell through after the death of their committee chairman, Ralph Matkin. Alan Smith asked me if I'd like to be commercial manager just after I joined Warwickshire, and I started to think 'Someone's trying to tell me something here,' so I eventually took the job."

Although Warwickshire were amongst the first counties to see the need for increased commercialism in cricket, the Warwick Pool being the leading fundraiser of its type, they hadn't seen the need for a commercial manager until Cumbes' appointment. He says of his first tentative steps into the world of corporate sponsorship: "We had nothing to refer to, our attitude was that if we tried an approach and it worked, then great, but if it didn't, it was dropped."

Such a modest approach must have led to more good ideas than bad, because it wasn't long before his former club approached him, believing, not without just cause, that Jim Cumbes would be the ideal man to revitalise the commercial income of a football club during difficult times for the sport. "Villa asked me to do the job before Tony Stephens was appointed, during the mid-eighties. I turned them down, because the image of football wasn't great at the time and I thought I'd be better off at Edgbaston. Then, when Tony left to work for Wembley, they asked me to be his replacement. I thought about it again, but by now Warwickshire were doing well on the commercial side and I was enjoying myself, so I turned it down again.

"I might have left if I'd known how football would take off, but in 1987 Lancashire asked me to move to Old Trafford to become their first commercial manager. By now I thought the time was right to make a move; Warwicks had a new chief executive and I'd been a bit disappointed not to get the job. I'd never given much thought to going back to Old Trafford before then, but when I was approached it was such a big opportunity that I fancied the idea."

Cumbes spent ten years as Lancashire's commercial manager, before becoming chief executive in 1997. "John Bower left, and I was asked to take over temporarily. Then I was offered the position permanently; I was stunned, and I had to think about whether I wanted the promotion. I was enjoying life in the commercial department, but I had to think about the future and how I would get on with any other new boss, so I accepted."

In Cumbes' time in charge of Lancashire, cricket has undergone a transformation that, while it may not have been as high-profile as the commercialisation of football, has nevertheless transformed the game and helped set the scene for England's Ashes triumph during the summer of 2005. After having won honours at both sports and now running not only one of the best-known clubs in cricket, but also one situated in the shadow of the world's self-proclaimed biggest football club, Cumbes is the perfect man to comment on the changes made to a game struggling to prosper in the glamourous shadow of football.

It can't be easy to compete with a neighbour who will attract more customers to their club shop on a non-matchday than Lancashire will see during the four days of a Championship game, but Jim remains as ebullient as ever he has during any aspect of his working life. "Cricket moves on, but being involved day to day you don't really notice it. We've been looking at the possibility of moving to a new ground, but we first thought about the idea eighteen months ago and we're still talking about it. If we don't move we've got to transform the existing ground and make it fit for the 21st century."

And not only do the grounds change. Cricket has received a welcome shot in the arm with the success over the past couple of years of the floodlit 20/20 games. Cumbes is well aware of the boost in income this type of cricket brings, whilst also aware of the feelings of the cricketing purists. "We played Yorkshire in the summer of 2004. We thought we might get a gate of six or seven thousand, yet on the night there were 15,000 here. We need those type of gates; the days when we'd get over thirty thousand a day for county games have gone. Some of our members might not have liked the idea but there's been some good cricket played. The successful sides play 'proper' cricket, it's just a bit faster.

"Getting someone into cricket's like getting them into music. The other night I was on my way home and the guy on reception was playing a Frank Sinatra song. He told me that he'd got into Sinatra because of Michael Bolton. That's like cricket; you have to get into the easy stuff, the 20/20 and the limited overs, and then you can be converted to the four-day game. Same with football; you watch the Champions League and the Premiership on television, then you might start to enjoy watching a team lower down the scale and playing yourself. Kids don't play and then watch, it's the other way round. When I was a kid, we'd watch the cup final, then go out and play ourselves."

Married with a son and a daughter, Jim lives in Altrincham where he also writes a column for the Manchester Evening News and makes occasional after-dinner speeches – another job for which he needed little training. If anyone was a born raconteur, it's the former Runcorn Town, Tranmere Rovers, West Bromwich Albion, Aston Villa, Portland Timbers, Southport, Coventry City and Worcester City goalkeeper, Warwickshire, Lancashire, Surrey and Worcestershire fast bowler, Warwickshire and Lancashire commercial manager, market trader, shop-keeper, Radio Birmingham disc jockey, packer, driver, key insurance salesman and now Lancashire chief executive. In any case, he probably couldn't have spared the practice time.

AT THE BACK

George Curtis

Respect is a word often bandied about without justification, particularly in the hype-ridden world of professional football. However, there are some men in the game for whom being respected comes naturally, whether by talent, achievement or by sheer force of personality.

George Curtis is one such figure. A loyal servant to Coventry City as they climbed the divisions during the sixties, his success upon returning to help guide the club to FA Cup success two decades later could not, it was agreed by common consent, have happened to a nicer man.

Yet Curtis commands respect for more than his footballing achievements. I first saw him outside Highfield Road, before a Coventry match. A badge seller had set up his stall in what was the most beneficial position to maximise his sales. Unfortunately it was just outside the entrance to a sponsors' lounge and George asked, politely, if the seller would move. As he was in a public place, said purveyor of unofficial goods was well within his rights to refuse, and years of operating on the fringes of the law would doubtless have made him well aware of the fact. But he was happy enough to apologise, pack up and move to a less attractive spot. That's the type of respect George Curtis commands. You don't have to have seen him play to know that here is someone you want to be friendly with. Not that Curtis is in any way aggressive. Indeed, a more polite and well-mannered individual you'd have to travel a long way to find. He has the ability to make anyone around him aware that here is a man of some substance.

Born in Dover, in 1939, George left school to become a miner in the Kent coalfields, playing football for Snowden Colliery before attracting the attentions of a Coventry City scout. Such an uncompromising introduction to the world of work made him remember forever how lucky he was that football provided an escape route. "I'd been working down the pit for nine months when I was asked to go up to Coventry for a trial. I was taken on as an apprentice, and signed professional forms in 1959."

Joining Coventry at this time enabled Curtis to claim a record few players can emulate, and none will be able to match in the future. "I played in the Third Division South. Then when the regional leagues were scrapped Coventry had finished in the bottom half, so we went into the fourth division. I then played for them in every division from the fourth to the first."

Much of this dramatic rise was due to the arrival as manager in 1961 of Jimmy Hill. He came to Highfield Road after a successful playing career and was later to be involved with the Professional Footballers Association in the George Eastham court case that led to the maximum wage being abolished. Curtis was one of the players waiting eagerly for the benefits to be reaped. "I'd started on £8 a week, then when the maximum wage was abolished we were on £20. It was well-known that Fulham were paying Johnny Haynes £100, and we thought that we'd be getting some of that. But because he was a manager now, Jimmy still only paid us £20."

The small matter of wages apart, Coventry players had little to complain about as Hill's enthusiasm sent the team racing through the divisions, transforming a club that had previously been thought of as a footballing backwater into the most forward-thinking in the country. Curtis can still speak with obvious enthusiasm about this period. "Jimmy came in with Derrick Robbins as chairman and suddenly the place was completely different. They had so many ideas. Jimmy made sure that when we were coming from an away match we'd always stop off and have a drink. I asked him why and he said 'When they're drinking, they're talking. I find out if there's any problems when we're out'."

By now. Curtis was team captain. He proved to be such a model of consistency that he only missed a couple of games between first getting into the team and suffering a broken leg in 1967 during Coventry's initial season in the top flight, by which time Hill had left the club for a job in television. Of course, recovery was much different then than it is now. "I was going down to the training ground – another first for City, we were one of the first clubs to have our own purpose-built training ground – then afterwards I'd run back six or seven miles to Highfield Road for treatment on the broken leg."

Curtis was renowned throughout football as a hard man, the type of player who could hold his own during the era of Norman Hunter, Nobby Stiles and Tommy Smith. He insists, though, that his reputation was an undeserved one. "I was never a dirty player. In fact, I was only ever sent off once, and that was in a reserve game when I was sixteen. I was fouled, and as I got up I started swearing at the other fella, telling him was I was going to do to him. The referee called me over and said 'No you're not, son. You're going off.' And that was that. Players nowadays, they're stupid. They'll foul their opponent and then stand there waiting for the referee to see them. We'd do it and then we'd be thirty yards away before anyone noticed that something had happened."

Curtis made a full recovery from his injury and regained his place in the first team, but by late 1969 his time at Highfield Road was coming to an end. Tommy Docherty's Villa side had got off to a bad start in what was expected to be a promotion-challenging season, and the Doc thought George Curtis was the man to help him out in a crisis. A fee of £30,000 was paid and after 539 games, still a Coventry record for an outfield player, during which time he scored 13 goals, George was on his way to Villa Park in December 1969. "At his best when things aren't going smoothly" was the Docherty assessment of Curtis's abilities, although the Villa manager of the time had little opportunity to reap the full benefit. Curtis scored in his Villa debut, away at Swindon on Boxing Day, and for good measure scored Swindon's goal in a 1-1 draw, but form continued to slide and Docherty was sacked the following month. Of his transfer to Villa, George says, "I was coming to the end of my career, and I didn't have to move house. It was a good move for me."

Vic Crowe was installed in the manager's office but Curtis, by now team captain, suffered none of the problems of being a previous manager's signing. "There was no resentment either toward Vic from the players, or from him to me. We got on with our jobs and things got better from then on." Crowe had been unable to prevent relegation, but the two seasons spent in the third division proved to be vital in reviving the club's fortunes. Curtis, who had said on his arrival that, "There's nothing I love more than a battle," played a full part in this time, although he missed the 1971 League Cup final against Spurs with a cartilage injury. "One or two players had problems with the crowd. They were getting on Ray Graydon's back when he first arrived, and I said to him, 'When it starts, hold your hand up. They'll know you can hear them and they'll stop. That's the way they work. In any case they're paying your wages, so who's the fools?'"

Fittingly for such a brave player, George's career came to an end just as his last battle had been won, and in typical circumstances. "We were playing Notts County. During the first half Tony Hateley and I went into a challenge, and he broke my nose. Then he did it again in the second half and I needed an operation. I agreed that I wouldn't play unless it was strictly necessary, but in the final game of the season, at home to Torquay, when we'd already won the title, I broke it once more. The doctors said that I couldn't play for twelve months after that, so I retired. I didn't fancy ending my career slipping down the divisions." Curtis had played 57 games for Villa, scoring four goals. There have been longer Villa careers, but few players have given so much for the claret and blue cause. Then again, George Curtis knew no other way.

His playing career over, George was offered a job behind the scenes at Villa Park, but preferred to head back to the place he knew best. "Coventry offered me the job as commercial manager. Jimmy had left by then, but his ideas were still helping me. We'd seen how lotteries were making big money in America, so a few of us from the Midlands clubs went over there to see how they worked. That was a big money-spinner for us, and we had plenty of other ideas. Some worked, some didn't. I keep quiet about the ones that didn't."

Hill returned to Coventry as chairman in 1975, and a few years later came up with one of the more controversial ideas of the early eighties. In 1981 it was announced that Highfield Road was to be the first all-seater stadium in the country, and that away supporters were to be restricted to a small area, with tickets costing up to £6, at a time when home fans were paying as little as a third of that amount. Curtis is honest enough to admit that this novel idea wasn't a great success. "Looking back, supporters weren't ready for terraces to be scrapped. We should have kept a small area for those who would rather stand, as happened later. The pricing structure for away fans was also wrong. It just encouraged them to sit with the home fans, especially when we were playing local clubs such as Villa and Birmingham. It was all done with the best of intentions, but in the end it caused more problems than it solved."

Other ideas were more successful, and Coventry were able to defy gravity and stay in the top flight throughout the eighties, even though crowds dipped below 10,000 as football's myriad of problems during this period made marketing the sport a thankless task. "We brought in cheerleaders. Some people didn't like the idea, but it got them and their families into the ground. Three days a week we'd have players going out into the local factories. We'd make personal visits to sell executive boxes rather than doing it all over the phone. Arthur Pepper, who was my assistant, worked at organising trains and coaches to away games when other clubs didn't have anyone doing the job."

No matter how many ideas he may have thought up, though, Curtis's job would never be a total success. "The trouble was that Coventry would never have big money. When Jimmy was first there we had an overdraft of £1,000; the bank wouldn't let us have any more. Derrick Robbins probably guaranteed our debts, but we never had much to spend."

Hill had left the club for the second time in 1983, and the departure of Don Mackay as Coventry manager towards the end of the 1985-86 season saw George make what many thought was a long-overdue step. By now on the board as executive director ("Same job, different title."), he was asked to become manager, with John Sillett as his coach. "I insisted that I would be managing director, but although that was a sticking point with the rest of the board, they eventually agreed. I told them that the reason I wanted the title was because directors wouldn't be able to touch the team without seeing me first."

Under the joint command of Curtis and Sillett, the Sky Blues embarked upon the greatest season in their history. A final league place of tenth meant a rest from the usual relegation dogfight, and they rounded the campaign off when winning the FA Cup, thanks to a 3-2 defeat of Spurs in the final. The most enduring image of the day was of the club's managing director and chief coach, two of the most popular and best-loved figures in the game, standing on the Wembley turf holding up the famous old trophy. Yet for Curtis, winning the only major honour in Coventry's history was not the highlight of the season. "It was a great performance," he says, "but the league results over 42 games proved it wasn't a fluke."

The season over, Curtis found that he had been a victim of his own success. "John was a brilliant coach, and he wanted to be manager, which was fair enough. But my contract said that he couldn't take the job, so I agreed to retire and work back on the commercial side until I was 55. I helped John at times but I was happy to carry on as Executive Director again until I retired. Then I helped out on that side of things for a few years part-time, and eventually stepped down completely."

Still living near Coventry with his wife, George is content in semi-retirement. "I do a bit of driving for an agency, moving new cars round, that sort of thing. I work when I want to, and it suits me. I keep my hand in and it keeps me busy. I play golf four or five times a week. I do work for the SPARKS childrens' charity, and myself and my wife spend a lot of time in Majorca where we have a place."

One thing George Curtis doesn't do, which may come as a surprise, is to attend many football matches. "People always assume that I watch a lot of football, but I don't. I was never a great watcher, and there's nothing I can do at the game to influence how it goes, so I don't go."

Former players can also find it hard to settle into the role of being an ex-pro but Curtis seems happy enough. "Football was my job; people say I was lucky to have a job like that but it was just what I did for a living. I loved doing it but if you treat it as anything else it can run away with you."

John Gidman

John Gidman was Villa Park's ultimate seventies footballer. He looked and dressed the part, played his football in such a way as to make the deeply unglamorous position of right-back fashionable in the school playgrounds of Birmingham, and had several brushes with his club's management.

Born in Garston, Liverpool, in 1954, Gidman made what must have seemed a dream start to his career when being taken on as an apprentice with Liverpool straight from school. However, despite a move from the wing into defence, John was unable to make the grade at Anfield and, released from his apprenticeship, moved to Villa in 1971, playing in the successful FA Youth Cup winning team the following year alongside another star of the future, Brian Little.

Gidman established himself in the first team during 1973-74, and remained a first-team choice until his acrimonious departure in 1979, despite several incidents along the way. The first was the appointment as Villa manager of Ron Saunders, of whom more later. The second was the horrific accident on Bonfire Night 1974, which almost cost John both the sight of his right eye and his career.

He explains: "We were at Jim Cumbes' bonfire party. I remember talking to some guy – he was a QC or something like that – and we were chatting about the IRA bomb campaign. I heard someone say 'Don't turn round,' but of course I instinctively did, and a firework came towards me at about 80 miles an hour. It hit me straight in the eye and David Targett, the club doctor, got me to lie down and told me I was bleeding and had to go to hospital. I realised afterwards that he was calming me down; he already knew the full extent of what had happened.

"The inside of the eye was shattered, the iris never recovered. I was in hospital for six weeks, and if I hadn't been a professional sportsman I'd probably have had my eye removed. As it was, it never fully recovered and I virtually had to learn how to play football again."

Gidman missed almost six months of Villa's promotion push, making his way back into the team in the final week of the season. He became a mainstay of the side for the next four years and made one appearance for England, against Luxembourg in 1977. Then-national manger Don Revie described it as "the best international debut since Duncan Edwards" and inexplicably never picked Gidman again.

Two years later, the resentment which had built up between Gidman and his close friend Andy Gray on one side, and Ron Saunders on the other, exploded into open warfare. Gidman's opinion of Saunders has not been lessened by the passage of time. "He'd walk down Lovers Lane holding hands with himself," is Gidman's assessment of his former manager's attitude. "He'd arrived from Manchester City with a reputation for not getting on with his players and that's what happened all the time he was at Villa. He never liked players who were bigger than him; he thought that all the attention should be focussed on Ron Saunders. Look at that time when he wouldn't let Andy go down to London to pick up his Player of the Year awards. That after he's won Manager of the Year and insisted on being able to come off a club tour to pick it up. He had no respect for anyone else. And then after he left Villa he joined Birmingham City and Albion, of all clubs. Andy left because of him, I went as soon as an offer came in." Gidman had played 233 games for the Villa, scoring nine goals, when he moved in September 1979.

The offer had been from Everton, for £750,000, and Gidman was on his way back to Merseyside, as one of the few players who have been on the books of both clubs. The move didn't entirely work out, although not for the obvious reason. "Being an ex-Liverpool player wasn't a problem," he says. "I thought it would be a good idea to get out of the environment of Villa Park, with all the problems I'd been having there, and go back home. I settled at Goodison and yet I didn't, if that makes sense. The city was starting to feel the effects of recession, Everton were struggling. I was into my second season, then Gordon Lee got the sack and Howard Kendall stepped in. He didn't fancy me, and Ron Atkinson came in and took me to Old Trafford for £450,000 and Micky Thomas." Gidman played 64 league games for Everton, scoring twice, prior to his move to Old Trafford in 1981.

By this time, Gidman must have been wondering how bad his timing was. The departure of he and Gray from Villa Park had led to a power struggle off the field and Ron Saunders being able to build a team that began the climb to the summit of European domination almost straight away. Equally, Everton had become league champions within three years of Gidman's leaving. Yet he remains unimpressed by what he left behind. "Kendall was a lucky manager. Before that League Cup game at Oxford I was contacted by a journalist who asked me for a quote, because Howard was going to get the sack. I replied that I wasn't going to point the finger; he hadn't given me much of a chance so there was nothing I wanted to say about him. Then they got a draw, won the replay and it all went on from there."

Ron Atkinson, though, was more to Gidman's liking. "I loved my time at Old Trafford. Ron's got as much character as a vintage Bentley; he loves the way people fall for the Mr Bojangles image, how they think he's all champagne and cigars when he really drinks bacardi and coke. We had our ups and downs, but it would be impossible to get on with someone every day. He was a players' manager. He'd played the game, he knew how he wanted it played."

Under Ron Atkinson, Manchester United played some of the finest football of the mid-eighties, but were never able to win the league crown they regarded with obsessive zeal. Their best chance came in 1985-86, when the team won their first ten games to build what appeared an unassailable lead in the title race, only to fall away badly after Christmas. By this time, Gidman had suffered an ultimately career-damaging injury, in the third game of the season, away at Ipswich when, ironically, he was feeling at the top of his game. "We'd won the FA Cup at the end of the previous season, then on the opening day we'd beaten Villa 4-0. Against Ipswich, Ian Cranson got me with a tackle from behind. It was a terrible tackle, just straight into me, and I could never forgive him for it."

Gidman battled back to fitness, but found that he not only had to overcome a broken leg in order to win his first-team place back. "I was at the airport, my leg in plaster, and I met Kenny Dalglish. His words to me were 'Just marking your card, Ron's bought John

Sivebaek'. I got back into the team and John played in midfield for a while, but that was really the end for me at Old Trafford."

Frozen out of the picture at United after 95 games and four goals, the chance of resurrecting his career came to Gidman from a surprise quarter, as newly-appointed Manchester City manager Jimmy Frizzell saw him as the type of player needed to help City's relegation battle, in October 1986. "He came on the phone, and asked me if I'd sorted my contract out with United. I said we had an agreement that I could leave on a free, and I was off to Maine Road, just in time to make my debut for them, against United. Funnily enough, just before that I had the chance to go back to Villa, but they wanted me to sell all my businesses up in the north-west and move back to Birmingham. By that time I had too much keeping me up there, so I stayed for a while and City came in for me."

Gidman's spell at Maine Road was not a successful one, and Frizzell was soon replaced by former Norwich manager Mel Machin. "He had it in for me from the start," says Gidman. "It all went back to a game at Carrow Road when he was playing for Norwich and I took the piss unmercifully out of him, running him ragged and scoring from the halfway line. On his first day in charge I reminded him about it. I didn't last much longer." Gidman had played 53 games for City, scoring a single goal.

Gidman's next move saw him sign for Stoke City, also of the second division, in the summer of 1988. "Mick Mills was their manager, and when he first asked if I wanted to join them I told him, 'Fine, but don't expect me to play every match.' I was 34 and my career was catching up with me. I needed more rest between games, but the coaching staff's idea of having a day off was to get us running even more. I was there for a few months and played ten games, then Brian Little came in for me to go as player-coach at Darlington."

Linking up with that other great Villa icon of the seventies was to prove Gidman's swansong, as life at the bottom of the fourth division was tough in every way. "I was getting kicked to bits. Fit young nineteen year-olds were kicking lumps out of me, and I realised that this wasn't for me. Darlington went down to the Conference and money was even tighter than it had been before, so I thought it was time I gave up playing." It was now the summer of 1989, and Gidman had made 13 appearances for Darlington, to take his total of games in the Football League to 432. The single goal he scored at Feethams was the seventeenth of his league career, a surprisingly small number for a player who had made his name as one of the finest attacking full-backs in the country.

Gidman was to have one further role in the game: as player-manager of King's Lynn, in the Midlands Division of the Doc Martens' League. "Brian sorted me that job out. I thought I'd give it a go, maybe have a year or two there to see what I could do as a manager. I moved into the town and I was working at the job full-time, although the rest of the players were part-timers. We had a great start. I got Ron Atkinson to bring Villa over for a friendly to raise a bit of money, then suddenly my wages weren't being paid into the bank. This went on for a couple of weeks, and there was no money so I had to leave. They still owe me thousands, but I doubt I'll ever see any of it."

Already a successful businessman, with several concerns in Liverpool, Gidman had found himself involved in the murky world of politics as another investment turned out to be more complicated than had first appeared. "I arranged with Derek Hatton, who had just been involved with Militant and then kicked out of the Labour Party, to build a golf range on Merseyside. The idea was that we built it, ran it for a couple of years and then sold it on at a profit. Anyway, it opened – I didn't know at the time, but one or two people were aware that someone high up wanted Hatton taught a lesson. Then one Friday morning I was in bed with my wife and she says, 'There's someone at the door.' I got up to check it out, and there were two blokes with an axe, knocking down the front door. In all there was eight of them, real heavies from the Fraud Sqaud, come charging in. They had with them this computer I'd never seen before. They told me things about myself that I didn't even know. It turned out that my phone had been bugged, on the authority of the prime minister, Margaret Thatcher. They told me I couldn't speak to my wife, they made me put some clothes on in the toilet while two of them stood there. It was just like something out of James Bond.

"The reason they'd picked me up on a Friday was because they could hold me over the weekend. Eventually I was released on £1,000 bail, and that's when the fireworks started. They went through everything, my tax returns, all my businesses. My wife had a childrens' clothes shop, I'd just sold a sports shop and they wanted everything connected with those. The final meeting I had with the Fraud Squad was with two detectives in a bar. I insisted that they took their shirts off in the toilets so I could see that they weren't wired, which they weren't. They wanted to know all I could tell them about Derek Hatton; I was reluctant to say anything about him, and in the end all charges against me were dropped."

After an investigation lasting over three years, the trial of Derek Hatton and six of his associates took place at Chester Crown Court in 1993. Gidman, long-since cleared of all involvement in any wrongdoing, was no more than an interested observer, and that from a distance. "The police had told me to be out of the country while the trial was going on, so I went on holiday to Spain with my wife. All the accused were acquitted, and it seemed to me that all of us were guilty by association because someone was trying to get at Derek Hatton. It cost me, though; the case took so long to get to court and the pressure was so great on me that my marriage broke up and I ended up getting divorced."

By now, Gidman was looking at a broken marriage and businesses that had inevitably suffered due to the publicity of the fraud investigation. It was only natural that he began to see his future in terms of a completely fresh start. "After it was all over I went on holiday to Cuba with a friend of mine, Roy Chand. We'd been there for six weeks and I suddenly said, 'I'm off. I'm not staying at home'. He thought the sun had got to me and I'd forget all about it once we got back, but I'd made my mind up. I like the sun and the sea and there wasn't anything to keep me in England.

"I'd been to Spain a few times on football trips and then on holidays, so I booked a flight, intending to stay a few weeks and then travel around Europe. Eight years later, I'm still here. I put a deposit down on a place in Gijon, up in the mountains. Everyone told me I'd go mad up there on my own, but that was just what I wanted – to be alone to sort myself out. I was fed up with hangers-on. What had happened had shown me that I hadn't got many true friends. So I stayed here, met my girlfriend and settled down."

Gidman now lives in southern Spain, some 30 miles from Marbella. "I'm lucky in that I can live without football. It's hard when you give up playing – you miss all the things that go with it,

John Gidman

and some players can't live with that. I couldn't see myself staying in the game, though. You have to change your character when you become a manager. There's a chairman to answer to, which is something you don't have to do when you're a player. I'll always be too much of a rebel to have been a manager. It's in my blood."

And it helps that Gidman was wise enough at an early age to make provision for the day when he gave up the game. "When I first joined the Villa, John Hazell, who died recently, came up to me and said 'You're going to be a big name.' I didn't take much notice, but he got me to start a pension fund, and all through my career I kept putting money in there. That's paying out now, so I'm doing all right. I don't have to work, I'm enjoying life."

Dennis Jackson

"We were standing in the tunnel at Wembley, waiting to go out to be presented to the Queen, and their team came out of the dressing room. I looked down the line and they were all there – Duncan Edwards, Bobby Charlton, Tommy Taylor, Jackie Blanchflower, the lot. I turned to Doc Pace and said, 'We've got no chance here'." Luckily for Villa history, Dennis Jackson, right-back and narrator of this fascinating tale, played football a lot better than he made predictions.

Dennis was born in 1932, and when it came to the question of which football team he would support, the youngster had little choice in the matter. "I was born just off Lozells Road, around the corner from where Villa were founded. I went to Gower Street school, off Trinity Road, and I played table tennis for the Aston Cross Wesleyan Church."

Yet despite this upbringing, Dennis's first foray into the professional game was with Villa's traditional rivals West Bromwich Albion. "I left school when I was 14 and started work at Ansell's brewery, in the offices there, working with Charlie Tabberner who later became steward at the Lions Club. I was also on the ground staff at the Albion, training twice a week."

It was Dennis's enrolment in the army during National Service that was to prove a turning point in his football career. "I was stationed up in Manchester, and the Albion wouldn't pay my expenses to travel down when I was playing for the reserves. So I asked them to cancel my contract and got fixed up with Hednesford Town. I'd just come out of the army, in 1953, and I'd only played a couple of games when Arthur Corbett, who was Hednesford's manager, said the Villa were looking at me. One of the scouts, Ernie Savage, said he'd been impressed with the way I played and wanted me to turn out for Villa reserves the next week in a Midland Floodlit League match. We beat Port Vale, I did okay and Eric Houghton, who was the manager then, said he wanted to see me in another reserve match. That was against Albion, which was a bit awkward after I'd just left them, but we won that one as well, and I signed full-time as a professional."

For a lad brought up in Aston, signing for the Villa, especially under the auspices of the legendary Houghton, was a dream come true. "The day I signed those forms, I thought to myself, 'This is all I've ever wanted to do'. That was on the Friday, and the following Monday I was in the reserve team at Villa Park, against Bolton. I was right-back and Danny Blanchflower was having a game at right-half because he was coming back from injury. You couldn't ask for a better partner. Danny would never pass to you unless you were in ten yards of space."

Dennis was with Villa for over six years, but found himself restricted to just eight first team appearances, as the incomparable Stan Lynn made the number two shirt his own. "He was never out," recalls Dennis. "Never injured, never suspended, never had a bad game. I lost count of how many games he played on the trot. And he kept scoring goals as well. I was on the bench one afternoon when he got a hat-trick. I remember thinking when he got his third, 'That's me not getting a game for another six months'."

The highlight of Jackson's career at Villa Park was a place in the party that travelled to Wembley for the 1957 FA Cup final against Manchester United. "I said before the match that we'd got no chance, but from the kick-off we were on top, even before Ray Wood was injured. It was only in the last fifteen minutes that United started to attack us, and by then we'd got the match won. Eric and the trainer, Bill Moore, got everything right that day."

Jackson may not have received a cup-winner's medal, but he did leave Wembley with a consolation prize. "I'd been sitting on the bench next to Eric and Bill. When the match finished, Eric told me to run back to the dressing room and get the champagne ready to fill the cup. I got Doc Pace, who had missed out on a place in the team as well, to come and help me.

"Then, as we were sorting it all out, the players started to come back into the dressing room. Peter McParland put his shin pads down and I thought they'd make a nice souvenir, so I swiped them.

He knew all about it, but he's not getting them back. My son's got them now."

This brief flirtation with glory aside, Jackson spent most of his time at Villa Park in the reserves, which in itself was no mean feat considering the amount of players on the club's books, at a time when five or six sides were regularly fielded in various leagues. Numbered amongst the Villa Park ranks during this period was a young, amateur wing-half named Ron Atkinson. Big Ron well remembers the full-back with whom he played many a reserve game. "Dennis invented the banana shot," he recalls, before adding, with typical Atkinsonian humour, "The trouble was, he was trying to shoot straight at the time."

Unable to stake a regular first-team place, Jackson left Villa for Millwall during the summer of 1960 for a small fee. "Jimmy Seed had just left Charlton to join Millwall and he wanted me to sign for them. I travelled down, but we couldn't agree terms. The maximum wage was still in force so I wanted a few bob extra to make it worth my while moving to London. Jimmy refused to pay me, so I came back and started training with the Villa again. Then a couple of days later, Joe Mercer, who was managing Villa by then, came up to me and said that it was all sorted; Jimmy Seed was going to give me what I wanted and I should get the next train down to London. I went there, they had a taxi waiting for me at Euston, and I went straight to Jimmy's office at the Den. He opened a drawer in his desk, put his hand under the table and handed me the money I'd asked for. So it was a genuine under the counter payment."

While such payments were a strictly illegal part of the game, it would be pointless to deny that they existed. "It went on all the time, but I don't suppose the F.A. will bother about tracking me down now. I'd never had any real money, so I was grateful of the chance to make a few pounds."

The dockland surroundings at third division Millwall were a contrast to the aristocratic, if decaying, splendour of Villa Park, but Jackson settled in well. "I was made captain straight away, and I enjoyed myself there. We had a good side, and I was chuffed to be captain. We had an 18 match unbeaten run at the start of the season, another two games and we'd have taken Liverpool's record, but we lost 1-0 away at Notts County."

However much football has changed in the years since Dennis was captain of Millwall, one thing has stayed more or less the same. "Their fans were just as bad then as they were later on. They called me Stonewall Jackson, after the American general in the Civil War, and although they were great for us, they were terrible to the other team. We used to run out on to the pitch and even back then there was wire netting round the steps leading from the dressing room. They'd always be spitting at the opposition as they ran out – looking back, it was disgraceful. We used to kick off at 3.15 on Saturday afternoons, and it was always reckoned that the reason we started after everyone else was to give the dockers time to get from the pubs on the other side of the Thames into the ground."

Millwall were a perennial mid-table third division side, but still managed to attract decent crowds. "We'd be getting anything up to 30,000 for the big matches. We played Crystal Palace at Selhurst Park in the FA Cup and our supporters were getting into the ground any way they could: over walls, through fences, knocking down the gates. No matter what the official crowd was given as, there were well over 40,000 in the ground that afternoon. We played in the London Floodlit Cup against all the big teams – Arsenal, Chelsea, West Ham. They always hated coming to the Den, and there was always fights going on when they played there."

Jackson was at Millwall for four seasons, making 128 appearances, until the summer of 1964 saw a familiar, although unexpected, figure make a re-appearance into his football career. "Millwall's manager, Reg Smith, told me I had a visitor. I wondered who it might be, then in walked Eric Houghton. He was manager of Rugby Town, and he wanted me to play for him. He told me that he was signing Stan Crowther and Wally Hazeldene, who had both been at Villa, as well as some other big names. Even though they were in the Midlands Division of the Southern League, the money was better than I was getting at Millwall because Rugby had a chairman who was bankrolling them; I think he was the managing director of one of the big car firms in Coventry. Millwall agreed to let me go on a free, and I signed for Rugby. Some of the lads they signed got jobs for the car firm, but I was still a full-time player."

The Southern League of the period was the strongest non-league set-up in the country, featuring such clubs as Cambridge United and Oxford United, captained by Dennis's old Villa reserve teammate, Ron Atkinson. Jackson remembers: "It was a good standard of play. We were getting crowds of around 3,000 and we got promotion to the Premier Division, although we couldn't get into the Football League because there was no automatic promotion then, and it was pretty much a closed shop."

Jackson spent three years at Rugby, playing most of his 100+ games at right-back, although there was a time when he was pressed into service as an emergency forward. "We'd got some injuries, so I was stuck up at inside-left. I scored a few, as well." However, a knee injury failed to heal properly and he was forced to give up the game in 1967, at the age of 35. Dennis remains philosophical about the end of his playing career. "I'd had a good seventeen years in the game, which was a long time in those days."

Retirement from full-time football led to Dennis embarking on another sporting enterprise. "I bought a bookmakers shop in Park Road, Hockley. It used to belong to Jimmy Black, but I took it over and re-named it D.L.J. Turf Accountants. I owned that until 1971, when I sold out and went to work for Wimbush's the bakers, in Bordesley Green, as a van driver."

Working in such close proximity to St. Andrews must have caused some annoyance to a former Villa player, particularly one with such lifelong allegiances to his former club. "There was a load of Blues fans there and they used to give me some right stick. And every day I'd drive to work, see the big Wimbush advertising hoarding on top of the ground, and curse them."

Jackson endured such cruel and unnatural punishment for ten years before moving across the city to deliver cleaning supplies for a company based in Hockley. "I was there for fourteen years, and then I retired from work."

However, it soon became obvious that for Dennis Jackson, there was a world of difference between retirement and not working. He had turned out for the Villa Old Stars on a few occasions after his retirement from the full-time game, and took over managing the team in 1989. Dennis handled this role until 2004, when former Villa player from the late sixties, John Chambers, who had made a successful career in management on the local non-league scene, took over.

Dennis says of his period in charge of what is now the longest-running former players team in the world, "There was a long time when things weren't run properly. We'd struggle to put a team out. We'd have players who had never played for the Villa; on a few occasions we had to bring in friends of some of the players to make up the numbers. It was hard to raise a proper team. Then the club began to take an interest, and when Neil Rioch got involved and helped to found the Aston Villa Former Players' Association, things started to take off."

Now living almost within the sound of the Villa Park crowd, at Perry Barr, and the father of three sons who are, naturally, all Villa supporters, Dennis remains treasurer of the Villa FPA and also works for the club in a hosting capacity on matchdays. "Anything I can do to help, I will," are the understated words of a man whose passion for the club is now into its eighth decade.

Ivor Linton

Many changes have taken place in football over the past thirty years. Some have been, to put it kindly, a mixed blessing, although the virtual eradication of racism from the English game is one development that any right-thinking individual will applaud. A multi-racial Premier League team is no longer cause for comment, and for that reason alone, a debt of gratitude is owed to the black players who were brave enough to play at a time when they suffered sickening abuse, often with little protection from the game's authorities, and when far-right groups considered football a fertile recruitment ground. The likes of Cyrille Regis and Laurie Cunningham at West Brom gained most of the plaudits for their part in this breakthrough, but each club had at least one player who fought with similar bravery.

Ivor Linton was one of the promising crop of youngsters who came through the Villa youth scheme during the late seventies. Although his first-team career was limited, Linton's name is remembered in a number of ways. As the club's first British-born black player, Ivor played a significant role in acting as an inspiration for the multi-racial areas around Villa Park, showing that the region's biggest football club was not an exclusively white preserve.

He also took part in a couple of pieces of Villa Park folklore. It was Linton who was replaced by Robert Hopkins in the game against Norwich in 1980, when Hopkins came on as a substitute and scored with his only kick of the match. And one of Linton's final appearances in claret and blue was the dramatic European Cup second round tie in Berlin, when Tony Morley scored one of the greatest goals in the club's history.

Born in West Bromwich, in 1959, Ivor signed apprentice forms with Villa despite competition for his signature from several clubs, including Manchester City, who he had originally decided to join, and Albion, the team he followed. "I was going to City, then Villa stepped in and I don't know why, but I changed my mind and said I'd join them. Albion came for me, they even sent a scout to stand outside the classroom at school waiting for me, to try to get me to join them, but I fancied Villa."

Linton made a total of 17 full appearances for Villa, first as a midfielder and then at right-back, the position in which he played in Berlin. Despite appearing in the 1978 FA Youth Cup final against Crystal Palace and being called into the England under-18 squad ("Ron Saunders pulled me out because I was needed for the first team"), Linton never managed to establish himself alongside such contemporaries as Colin Gibson and Gary Shaw, leaving Villa Park in the summer of 1982 to join Peterborough United, then in the fourth division. Of his short career at Villa, Linton is honest enough to admit, "I've only got myself to blame. I was always a bit too laid-back. Ron Saunders gave me plenty of chances, but I never had the right attitude."

Peterborough were then under the management of Martin Wilkinson and it was here, in one of the game's less celebrated outposts, that Linton began to enjoy his football again. "Martin was a great boss. He put me back into midfield, playing off the front two, which I enjoyed. He taught me a lot and he gave me a lot of confidence. Peterborough was a lovely city to live in, everyone was so friendly and I really enjoyed my time there.

"Racism wasn't that much of a problem, either. Despite it being a much less multi-cultural place than Birmingham, I never had any trouble. I'd noticed racial abuse at the bigger grounds in the first division, and maybe at one or two away grounds after I moved, but at Peterborough there was hardly anything at all and the only time it ever bothered me was when family or friends came to watch and I was worried that they might hear something."

Unfortunately, as is often the case, a new manager came along who was to have a detrimental effect on Linton's career. "John Wile took over, and we didn't hit it off. He might have been one of my Albion idols when I was younger, but that didn't count for anything once I was playing for him. I had a two-year contract but I didn't get the chance to see it out before I was away." Linton had played 27 games for Peterborough, scoring three goals.

In fact, the next move was something of a step-up, albeit an unusual one. Ron Saunders was now in charge across the city, and remembered the versatile midfielder-cum-right-back to whom he had first given a chance at Villa Park. Ivor was off to join the growing ex-Villa colony at Birmingham City who were then fighting what would prove to be a losing battle against relegation from the old first division.

"I didn't have much of a problem with the fans, despite my Villa connections. As far as they were concerned I was another new player, and I suppose that if they'd accepted the manager who won Villa the league then they wouldn't mind a player who'd only been in the first team a few times."

Linton spent much of the 1983-84 season at St Andrews, playing just four games for the first team. Not only was he attempting to avoid relegation but he also witnessed at first hand the antics off the field of his team-mates. A group of Blues players, centred around Linton's former Villa colleagues Noel Blake and Robert Hopkins, were becoming notorious around the city for their behaviour.

That professional footballers behaved in such a way was surprising enough. That the arch-disciplinarian Ron Saunders permitted such goings-on from his charges remains a source of wonder to this day. Ivor, though, has his theories. "They got away with it time and again. Every time you thought that Saunders would come down on them, he left alone. But he liked them. You could see the fear on the faces of the opposition when we were playing – Mick Harford terrorising defenders, Noel Blake charging in.

"I'm sure that Saunders let them get away with everything they did because he thought it helped them build that spirit on the pitch. They were playing for their club and they gave their all. The times were different than, as well. Football wasn't as popular, so people weren't that bothered about what footballers got up to. Whatever they did usually managed to stay out of the papers, and I can't see that happening these days. "

Things didn't work out at St Andrews for Linton, and he soon found himself on the move once more. "It was my fault again. The manager had given me another chance and I didn't make the most of it. I've got nothing but respect for the man, we had our fall-outs but he was great to me."

As an Albion supporter who moved to Villa, and then a former Villa player who signed for the Blues, Ivor Linton was obviously never one for taking life easy. But his next move was potentially the most fraught of the lot, as he explains. "I was looking for another club. Bradford City asked me to join them, but I fancied the idea of moving abroad. I could have played in Germany but instead, for some reason, I ended up in Finland."

As that rare commodity, a Black Country-born footballer playing in the Finnish league, Ivor was once more blazing a trail, albeit one that has not, at least as far as extensive research has shown, become well-trodden. He spent a season with LBK, two years with KIK, then joined Narpes Kraft and stayed there for 12 seasons, finally calling an end to his playing career in 1998 at the comparatively advanced age of 39. "Finland is a beautiful place. It's cold for a lot of the year, of course, but it's clean and very nice. I spent most of my time living in the Swedish-speaking part of the country, which is where I played my football. The people there are more Swedish, and they're more outgoing than those in the Finnish-speaking areas."

Football in Finland was still comparatively unrecognised during Linton's early time in the country, but gradually became better known. "When I arrived there were some good players in the league, but the big clubs in Europe wouldn't look at them. Finnish players had a reputation for being skillful, but not physical enough. Then Jari Litmanen did well with Ajax, and once one player came though, the scouts arrived looking for others. Jari was followed by Sami Hyypia and the goalkeepers, Peter Enckleman and Anti Niemi.

"The Finnish league was a bit different from playing in England, as well. The season was shorter, starting in early May and ending in October. Sometimes we'd play on Saturday and Sunday, while ten-hour journeys to away games were common. If we were lucky we'd fly, but often we'd leave on the Thursday, set up a training camp near to where we were playing, and have two league games at the weekend."

Ivor settled in Finland, living in the village of Overmark and raising two children, a boy and a girl. "The population of the village was about two thousand, it was a world away from West Brom. And the people were so reserved – they never seemed to notice that a

Ivor Linton

black footballer from overseas was living there." Indeed, so well acclimatised to life in Finland did Linton become that the question arose of his becoming a Finnish citizen and representing his adopted country at international level. "I was all for that, then someone pointed out that if I was to become a naturalised Finn I wouldn't just be eligible for the Finland team, but for national service as well. I suddenly went off the idea."

With his football career coming to a close, Ivor realised that he would have to find a second career to fall back on. "I'd studied to become an electrician while I was over there and, once I qualified, I started working for a couple of companies. From the age of about 36 I was a part-time footballer who also worked as an electrician, then three years later I decided to pack in playing. I could have gone on for another season, but I thought that it was about time I called it a day, and so I got a real job."

Linton stayed in Finland until 2001 then, after splitting with his Finnish-born partner, decided to return home. Ever the unwitting adventurer, he chose to return on September 11th. "I missed all the security scares by minutes. I was in the air when the planes crashed, and I landed at Heathrow just before everything went haywire. It makes you wonder, when you realise that you were flying at exactly the same time as all those people were being killed."

Back home in West Bromwich, Ivor has now severed virtually all links with the game he served for so long. "I work for a local firm of electrical contractors, travelling around the country. When the people I work with find out I was a footballer, they always ask me the same question: 'I bet you wish you were playing now, with all the money they earn, don't you?' But you know what? I don't think I do. I don't begrudge them their wages, good luck to them. I enjoyed my time and I was lucky to play for so long.

"I do feel strongly that the players I played with, the likes of Gordon Cowans and Tony Morley, didn't earn a lot. Has there ever been a Villa player since they were in the team who could touch either of them? I don't think so, yet there have been plenty since then who have made a fortune. But I don't think about football much now. I've watched the Albion maybe twice in twenty years; I see the Villa very rarely, but other than that I don't even watch football much when it's on television. I keep in touch with a couple of the players I was with at Villa and I turn out for the Old Stars occasionally, but that's it."

And indeed, should there ever be another chapter in the Linton sporting story, it will almost certainly come in an entirely different way. Ivor's daughter recently represented Finland in the World Junior Athletics Championships, running in the 4x100 metres relay in Italy and her father speaks with obvious pleasure of her achievements. "I don't know what the standard of sprinting is in Finland, but she ran for her country which made me very proud. I wonder whether she's got the dedication to have a successful career, though; sometimes she seems a bit laid back. I can't think where she gets that from."

Ian Ross

Ian Ross remains one of that select band of footballers to have captained an Aston Villa trophy-winning side. To narrow things down even further, he is one of just four men who have led the Villa to success in a Wembley final – the others, for the benefit of those less historically-informed, being Johnny Dixon, Kevin Richardson and Andy Townsend. For an encore he led the club to promotion back to the first division during the same 1974-75 season as he lifted the League Cup trophy. Yet 'Rossco,' as he was known to supporters and team-mates alike, remains a somewhat overlooked figure in the club's history. Indeed, forgotten hero might be an epithet that would describe Ian Ross perfectly.

When I first spoke to Ian, we arranged to meet a few days later at Liverpool's Lime Street railway station. I had a momentary worry during the journey, when I wondered if I'd recognise someone who I'd last seen almost three decades earlier – and then from a distance and in much different circumstances. It was, indeed, doubtful that Ian would be waiting on the station platform wearing the shirt he wore to collect the League Cup in 1975, claret and blue scarf draped around his neck. As it turned out, my fears were unfounded. He may not agree, but Ian Ross hasn't changed a great deal from the days when he captained Aston Villa. The hair may be thinner, but there's still a quiet assurance about the man that marks him out as someone you would notice in a crowd, even if you weren't sure of the reason why.

Born in Bishopbriggs, Glasgow, in 1947, Ian had an unusual football upbringing in this most fiercely partisan of cities. "I supported Partick Thistle. Not many of us did, but they were the first team I saw play. We lived near Thistle's ground at Firhill and one day (it must have been pre-season because the weather was glorious and Thistle never played in Europe in those days) I was there when they played Newcastle. It was a lovely night. I enjoyed myself and I was a 'Jags' supporter from then on."

Leaving school at the age of 15, Ross embarked on what was, for such a talented footballer, a mundane dream. "I always wanted to be a joiner. My elder brother was in the trade and he always seemed to have plenty of money, so that's what I wanted to be. I became an apprentice when I left school, but a couple of years later I was playing junior football when a few clubs came in for me."

'A few clubs' is how Ross describes the queue wanting to obtain his services. A better description might be 'a list of legendary names'. He explains, "Tommy Docherty fancied me to sign for him at Chelsea, as did Billy Wright who was managing Arsenal at the time; but Bill Shankly was the boss of Liverpool so nobody else had any chance."

Ross joined Liverpool in their FA Cup-winning season of 1964-65 and was able to see at first hand the foundations being put in place for one of the most glorious eras English football has experienced. He recalls, "Everything you hear about Shanks was true. He was a colossus; he dominated the club. I was due to play against Ferencvaros in a European match. We'd won the home leg and I was in the team for the away trip, and I was absolutely terrified of getting on Shanks' wrong side. I told Ian St John how I felt and he said 'That's not fear, it's respect'."

Despite seven seasons at Liverpool, Ross was unable to command a regular first team place, playing in just 48 league games and scoring two goals, although he did create something of a distinction in that these appearances were made in seven different positions in the team. "If I'd been anywhere else I might have been a regular, but Liverpool at that time were going through one of their phases where the team was 'Same as last year'. I think that in two seasons they only used about fifteen players in the first team, and remember, that was when they were playing about sixty games a season."

With no guarantee of first team football, Ian was willing to drop two divisions when the opportunity arose to move to Villa Park during the 1971-72 season, even though he found leaving Liverpool harder than anticipated. "The most I ever talked to Bill Shankly was the morning when Villa came in for me. He spent hours trying to persuade me not to go, but my mind was made up."

Ross had been on the verge of playing in enough games for Liverpool to guarantee a championship medal had the team won that year's first division crown, but despite this he was more than happy to join Villa. "I went to talk to Doug and Vic Crowe on the day Villa were due to meet Santos in a friendly and I got to meet Pele for the only time. If that wasn't enough to convince me of the club's ambition, when I signed it was the biggest fee a third division club had ever paid. That record lasted a week, then we bought Chris Nicholl. Villa were a great club – in fact, I've been lucky. I spent the best years of my career with well-run clubs."

Ross made his debut in a 2-0 win over Port Vale and quickly became a fixture in the Villa side, originally in midfield during the run-in to the third division title, and then settling alongside Chris Nicholl to form a central defensive partnership that, as with so much that characterised Aston Villa during those emotive days, brought a touch of first division attitude to the lower leagues. Two seasons of consolidation in the second division followed the promotion of 1972, during which time Ross suffered what was to prove the worst injury of his career. "Rikki Heppolette went over the top while we were playing Luton Town and sliced my shin open." And indeed, I can vouch for the fact that the Ross shinbone bears the scar to this day, a nasty testament to the downside of football. "We struggled while I was out. Maybe if I hadn't been injured we might have got promoted and Vic would have kept his job."

But Crowe was dismissed as, rightly or wrongly, it was felt by the board that he had taken Villa as far as he could. His replacement was, of course, Ron Saunders. By now, Ross was captain of the side, following the departure of Bruce Rioch to Derby County. "Ron realised that what he had inherited was quality. He'd had a bad experience with the players at Manchester City, but he knew that he was in control with us. He got the team playing football and, although we didn't start off too well, by the end of the season we'd have fancied our chances against any opposition, anywhere in the world. But we had to work for it. When he first arrived we thought he'd got us fit, but he just looked at us and said we were only halfway there."

As the season progressed, so Ross's captaincy became more important to a side beginning to really feel the pressure of the most success-hungry supporters in football willing them on. Chico Hamilton recalls how the team's captain did so much to ensure the season ended in triumph. "Ian was a smashing player and a great captain. He led us by example; not a great shouter but he was always there."

The League Cup final against Norwich will never feature long in the memories of anyone except Villa supporters, but the captain of the side who took the trophy as a result of Ray Graydon's only goal of the match smiles and says, "It was nice. But I got most satisfaction from the night at Hillsborough, when we won promotion. We won 4-0, I scored and there were all those Villa supporters there, packing the place out. Then we played Sunderland at home the following Saturday. There were 57,000 inside the ground with another 15,000 locked out, and we were back where we belonged."

With Villa in the first division, Ron Saunders set about dismantling the first of his successful teams, and Ian Ross found himself amongst the casualties. By the end of the 1975-76 season he had lost first the captaincy, and then his place in the side as Leighton Phillips began partnering Chris Nicholl in defence and the Villa central midfield gradually took on the appearance that would power the club to glory.

Ron Saunders agreed that Ross could move should another club make him an offer, but as the 1976-77 season continued, none appeared forthcoming. He recalls this time without rancour, "By that time I was only getting a game when other players were injured, so I went away on loan to get some matches in. I was with Notts County for a while; that was great, they were in the second division along with Forest and at that time it was County who were getting the bigger gates, until Brian Clough came along and changed things round a bit. Then I went to Northampton as a favour to Paddy Crerand, who was their manager. It was a bit strange, playing in the fourth division in front of a few thousand spectators, on a three-sided ground that they shared with the cricket team. But wherever you are in football, the dressing room's always the same."

After appearing in 205 games and scoring three goals for Villa, Ross was granted a free transfer in the summer of 1977. Like many other players of his era, he took time out to join the North American Soccer League. He failed, though, to share in the riches that stars such as George Best, Pele and Rodney Marsh attracted. "I was playing for Santa Barbara. It was a bit of a holiday. We were three hours drive from San Francisco, a couple of hours from Los Angeles. Disneyland wasn't far away, so the kids loved it. We weren't the best team in the world but I had a few good memories, such as the time I scored against Franz Beckenbaeur when he was with New York Cosmos. The trouble was that there was a problem with the club owner making promises he couldn't keep so we didn't get paid, but apart from that it was a good time."

Such minor hiccups as unpaid wages forgotten, Ross returned to join Peterborough United on a free transfer, under the managership first of Noel Cantwell, then John Barnwell. "I had a good time at Peterborough. We were getting crowds of between six and eight thousand, we were doing steadily in the third division. I enjoyed myself, the players were a good bunch of lads and I did okay." In fact, Ross did so well that he and his defensive partner Chris Turner were named in the PFA third division team of the season for 1977-78. His sojourn into one of football's backwaters was ended in the summer of 1979, after 122 games and a solitary goal, when manager Barnwell took charge of Wolves and invited Ian to join the backroom staff at Molineux. "I was reserve team coach, and I played a few games for them as well. I was instrumental in getting Emlyn Hughes to sign – he was all set to join Manchester City, so I drove up to Formby one Sunday lunchtime, to the pub I knew he'd be in, and talked him into signing for us.

With Hughes in the side and Andy Gray bought from Villa for what was briefly a world transfer record of just under £1.5 million, Wolves briefly looked set to enter the big time. However, despite winning the League Cup in 1979-80, the Molineux good times were destined to go into reverse, as Ian explains. "John started off well at Wolves, but looking back, they were spending money they didn't have. Andy and Emlyn were good lads, they were experienced pros, but they knew when to work and when to enjoy themselves."

John Barnwell had left and his place taken by Ian Greaves by the time Wolves' financial problems led to the brief chairmanship of Doug Ellis in the summer of 1982, to be followed by administration and the arrival of the Bhatti brothers, in a consortium fronted by Molineux legend Derek Dougan. Ross, by this point first team coach, recalls, "I knew that I wouldn't like the new set-up, so I decided to resign. Ian (Greaves) told me it was the worst decision I'd ever make. Then just a few weeks later the phone rings and he's on the line telling me that they'd sacked him."

Ross's time at Molineux did provide him with his first taste of management. "John Barnwell had been sacked. The first game, we were away at Liverpool, and it was the first time I'd ever sat in the directors' box. We were a goal up and Harry Marshall, who was the chairman then, leaned over with about ten minutes to go and said to me 'Good team selection you've made here'. I hardly had time to tell him not to talk so fast when, bang-bang. We were 2-1 down. That was Anfield for you. Then our next game was away at Arsenal and we lost again. I didn't get the job permanently."

Ross then found himself in another footballing outpost, and one that was even further away than Peterborough. "I was offered the job of manager of Valur, in Rekjavik. It was great – the season only lasts six months so I spent the summer in Iceland and the winter back home. The standard of football was surprisingly high; look at how many Icelandic players are making it in the game now. You could see that starting when I was there"

Four seasons saw Valur win the Icelandic title twice and finish runners-up on the other two occasions before Ross returned permanently to England. "My family wanted to. They enjoyed themselves out there, my children went to the US Embassy school, but it wasn't fair to keep uprooting them. I was able to come back to England and start taking my lad to games. He repaid me by becoming a Manchester United fan."

In 1985, Ross took the position of first-team coach to Eoin Hand at Huddersfield. "He was sacked after a short while and I was asked to take the job. I wouldn't do it as caretaker so they gave me the job permanently. We did well at first, and only just missed out on the play-offs, but after that we lost our way a little bit and when a new chairman came in, I was surplus to requirements."

Ross then moved back to Iceland, where he led KR of Rekjavik to runners-up spot in the league for two seasons in succession before returning to England as reserve team coach at Sunderland. "Peter Reid became manager and I knew he'd want to bring his own team in with him. I decided I'd had enough of football so I got out of the game entirely." Ross took the traditional former footballer's career path, opening pubs in the Cheshire village of Pinton and then in Altrincham. "I was in the trade for six years, which was more than enough. I'd always enjoyed a drink but I was never a big pub-goer. I was happy enough running the places, and we used to get a lot of Villa supporters coming in when they were playing games in Manchester, but by about 1998 I thought that the time was right to leave."

Living on the Lancashire coast, and with a grown-up son and daughter, Ian Ross is enjoying his retirement immensely. "First thing I do every morning is to take the dogs for a long walk. I spent a lot of time renovating my house, and one thing my wife and I really enjoy is travelling the world. It was something that football helped with; we had a family holiday in Australia in return for me doing some coaching out there, and when I was at Villa, Doug was always sorting us out with tours and end of season trips. We went to Martinique, to Africa, on Caribbean cruises. That gave me the taste for it and we've been lucky enough to carry it on. I'm enjoying what I do and I hope I'll be able to continue doing it for many years."

Shaun Teale

Born in Southport, in 1964, Shaun Teale first joined Everton as a YTS trainee, although his dreams of Goodison Park stardom were soon to be dashed. "Gordon Lee was my first manager, then Howard Kendall came in. By the middle of my second year he'd said I wasn't what they were looking for. It was hard to be told that I was wasn't wanted at Goodison, but it made me determined to get back into football."

The long road back into the professional game saw Teale start out at Ellesmere Port in the North-West Counties League before moving to Southport in the Conference. "I was working full-time in a shoe shop in Southport at the time, and I did the rounds of the non-league sides of the area. I just couldn't settle anywhere until I found myself at Northwich Victoria towards the end of 1986-87. I had the following season there, then they transferred me to Weymouth in the Southern League. It was a long way, but the big attraction was that my new club had a good record in bringing players into the league. Andy Townsend and Tony Agana had just left them; Graham Roberts had been at Weymouth as well. They bought me for £25,000 and I did well enough for Bournemouth to come in for me a year later. I cost them £90,000 at a time when the non-league record was only £100,000."

Teale spent two seasons at Bournemouth, playing in exactly 100 league games and scoring four goals, until Ron Atkinson gave him a second stab at the big time – a £300,000 fee making Shaun one of Big Ron's first Villa Park signings. "Suddenly I was in a whole new ball game. Villa were massive; there was my debut at Sheffield Wednesday, Ron's first match and it was back at the club he'd just left. He was desperate to win. The atmosphere was hostile up there but to be fair, he took it all on the chin and although we went two down we got a 3-2 win."

Teale settled into his role in the centre of Villa's defence immediately, although he is the first to acknowledge that his job was made easier by partnering the greatest defender of the time. "Paul McGrath. Brilliant. That's all you can say about him. Positioning-wise he taught me everything. He'd sometimes be caught out of position because he wasn't the quickest, then he'd do that back-heel he taught himself and he's won the ball. We'd run out together on to the pitch and we'd look at each other and say 'We'll do this our way'. Ron would be bawling instructions and one of us would put our hand up to show him we'd heard, then we'd carry on doing what we wanted."

If McGrath was the epitome of quality, another of Shaun's teammates, Les Sealey, provided memories of a different sort. "He was barmy. When I first joined the Villa I was a bit worried about who I'd be sharing a room with, because I smoked. We get to this tour in Germany; I find out I'm sharing with Les, so I go into the room a bit apprehensive – and he's there with a big cigar in his mouth."

Teale himself was certainly held in high esteem by his fellow professionals, while Martin Swain, covering Villa at the time for the *Express & Star*, is of the opinion that, "Villa wasted some money during the nineties. But I'd put Ron's signing of Shaun Teale in the top five transfer deals of the decade. He cost hardly anything and for two seasons was as consistent a defender as any in the league."

The 1992-93 season is fondly remembered by Villa supporters for the quality of the football, even though the team failed to win the inaugural Premier League title their play so richly deserved. Teale has vivid recollections of what went wrong. "We were going great, then suddenly there were three matches where we never performed. The Coventry nil-nil, which everyone talks about as being 'the Sheffield Wednesday day', because of what was happening up at Old Trafford when they lost in injury time. We got beaten 3-0 at Blackburn, where Sid Cowans tore us to pieces. Then the final match at home against Oldham. We blew it there and United went tearing past us."

Villa's blow-up in the final stages of the season gave support to the theory that Atkinson, tactically astute though he may have been on the big occasions, lacked the all-round managerial ability to win the title. Teale agrees with this synopsis. "He wasn't tactically aware enough; he was great with players as long as they were good for him."

Atkinson was certainly clever enough to know how to counter Manchester United the following season at the climax of a Coca-Cola Cup run that remains Teale's greatest footballing memory. "There were the two legs against Blues, with Bossie saving a penalty and Paul Tait putting Rico into the crowd. Then there was that night up at Sunderland: Bossie pulled off all those saves and we had four attacks, but we won 4-1. We beat Arsenal, when I had to play left-back, and they hadn't lost a cup-tie for two years. Ron got the tactics spot on that night. Earl Barrett marked Ian Wright and Wright never got a kick. Earl could have been a great player, but he was signed as a replacement for Macca and Macca wouldn't go. So Earl was shifted to right-back and didn't really make a success of it.

"Then there was Spurs on a horrible night when they had Sol Campbell up front. And Tranmere – what a tie that was. I was suspended for the first leg, when we got a hiding; then that second leg at Villa Park. The music was pumping, they were hanging from the rafters. Deano scored early on, I got the equaliser when Ray Houghton's leapt on me after I scored, then they scored the penalty and Dalian got our third with seconds left. There was a half-hour non-event called extra-time, and we went through with Bossie making those saves again.

"It took about half an hour to get off the pitch. The supporters were coming from everywhere, trying to grab bits of our kit. They'd hoist you on their shoulders, carry you, drop you and another load would dive on top."

The final, against Manchester United, was Ron Atkinson's finest hour. His tactics, to play Dean Saunders as a lone striker with Tony Daley and Dalian Atkinson attacking from the wings, worked perfectly. However, by this time the manager's relationship with the rock of his defence was beginning to crumble, as Shaun relates. "Earlier on in the season, we'd been playing Southampton and I smashed my nose on Ian Dowie's head. It was so bad that it had damaged the internal bone, so it bled constantly – in fact, when that happens you can bleed to death. Ron made me travel up to Liverpool shortly afterwards, even though I knew I wouldn't be playing. I got to the hotel and I was so ill that I went straight to bed and my brother-in-law had to come up to collect me and take me home. From then on I never looked at Ron in the same way.

"At the end of the 1993-94 season I was named in the England squad, but Ron pulled me out because he said I was injured, although he then made me go out to South Africa for a friendly. It was agreed that I could go on holiday, then have an operation to get my nose fixed and start pre-season training a couple of weeks later than most of the players. So I've had the op, then on the first day of training Jim Barron, Ron's assistant, rang me up and wanted to know where I was. I stood my ground, but of course all the backroom staff stuck up for the manager and made me out to be in the wrong."

The beginning of the 1994-95 season had seen Atkinson under fire for the amount of time he'd spent in the USA for that summer's World Cup, and the comparative lack of new signings. Teale agrees with the oft-mentioned criticism of the manager's last weeks at Villa. "He'd taken his eye off the ball. He was more interested in his television work," is his view of how Atkinson's priorities had altered.

Ron left Villa Park and although supporters were, on the whole, against the sacking, his departure was met with relief in one quarter at least. "I'd gone on the transfer list by then. Ron had got his inner circle who were undroppable, and whenever he had a go at them you knew he was just going through the motions." Indeed, Atkinson, in his autobiography *Big Ron – A Different Ball Game*, mentions an incident that had spoilt the run up to the Coca-Cola Cup final, where a story had been published claiming that the Villa players were unhappy with the choice of tailor for their cup final suits. Atkinson laid the blame at the feet of Teale's wife, Carol, but the player himself is adamant that this accusation is wide of the mark. "He knew who did it. It was two of his favourites, though, and he couldn't have a go at them. He had to find stuff for his book, and it was easier to blame someone else for his failings."

Brian Little took Atkinson's place and, although the team struggled, Teale was enjoying himself again. "I came off the list and although I played every game from then on, the team was playing poorly. Then, during the summer, I was talking about a new contract when Brian got me and my agent into his office and said he was 99% certain that he would be buying Chris Coleman from Crystal Palace.

He was as good as gold. He said that he didn't want me to go, but he understood that I might want to leave because he couldn't guarantee first-team football, and if I did want to go he'd try to get me out as cheaply as possible so that I could sort the best deal for myself. I was 31 by then, and I knew there wasn't much chance of a Premiership club coming in for me. When the pre-season friendlies started in August 1996, I was on the bench, with Gareth Southgate playing in defence. Tranmere came in for me and although it was dropping down a division, it felt right. I'd be going home and the money was ridiculous, much more than I was getting at Villa. In fact, I earned more in two years with Tranmere than in four with Villa."

Teale's five seasons at Villa Park had seen him clock up 176 appearances, testament both to his consistency and the club's ability during the period to engage in a few lengthy cup runs. He scored five goals, although he was renowned for always hitting the target whenever a penalty shoot-out was taking place

The traditional minnows of Merseyside football were enjoying their finest-ever period, finishing thirteenth and then eleventh in the first division during the two seasons Teale was a regular – and he was enjoying his football. "I had a good time there. But eventually John King, the manager, got the sack and John Aldridge took over from him. I'd had a double hernia operation and been pushed back into playing a bit too soon, and it was never right after that. Aldridge just didn't fancy me; for whatever reason, it wasn't happening, so I just drifted along. I went out on loan to Preston for a while, but nothing came of that."

With Teale's career in limbo, salvation came from an unexpected quarter. "I was asked if I fancied playing in Hong Kong. This was the summer of 1997, and I spoke to Mr Chang; the owner of Happy Valley. I worked it out that I would get as much as I was being paid at Tranmere, which was a lot more than the rest of the team would be on. It was a three month loan deal at first, so I told John Aldridge that they wanted to take me, but they'd only pay half my wages and Tranmere would have to pay the other half. He was happy with that, so I ended up with my Tranmere money from the Hong Kong team, and another half on top from Tranmere. I reckoned that I earned the bonus after the way Aldridge had messed me around."

Teale's three-month loan eventually stretched to a full year, playing in the Hong Kong league. "I was just on my way back home when the owner asked me if I was off on holiday. I explained the situation and he told me that I was under contract for twelve months and that he'd sue me if I didn't return. I was still a Tranmere player, so I came home and the next thing I knew was that he was phoning me to apologise and offer more money if I returned."

The Hong Kong league might have been a lucrative earner for Shaun Teale and several other English players, but the good times were not to last. "There were only two grounds in Hong Kong, the national stadium which held 30,000 and the Mon Koh which held about 8,000. We'd get crowds as low as two or three thousand for some games and maybe 15,000 when we played the top sides. We finished third in the league and won a cup, but the money was running out and they couldn't afford to keep me on for any longer."

Teale returned to England in summer 1998 to find his services once more in demand. "Motherwell contacted me. Harry Kampman was the manager, Brian McClair had returned and they were looking for a bit of experience in defence. They saw I was available on a free, asked me up there for a trial, and I got a contract."

However, life in the Lanarkshire steel belt was not all it could have been. "A hole" is how Teale describes Motherwell. "Just up the road was Larkhall, a big Rangers stronghold. I saw a man and a woman getting stabbed in the high street."

Teale spent two seasons in Motherwell as the club, like just about every other in Scotland, struggled to contend with life outside the Old Firm. "You'd have as many supporters going from Motherwell to watch Celtic or Rangers as came to see us," he said. In 2000, Teale's time at Fir Park came to an end after 45 games and three goals, amidst the type of controversy that might have been expected, as the madness of clubs throughout England and Scotland living beyond their means began to take its toll.

Shaun explains, "They'd brought in a lot of players and they were paying high wages. I was captain, Pat Nevin was player/chief executive, whatever that might mean. I'd been messed around in my second season: they'd made a few excuses about my new contract, and when we were in Portugal for the mid-season break we were hearing a few stories from the press about what was going on back home.

"Billy Davies, the manager by then, was in the papers saying 'If Shaun Teale thinks he's going to get that kind of money he's kidding himself'. I hadn't talked money at this point, I'd just wanted to know what was going on. Next day in the papers I caned the manger and the chairman. I called them both two-faced liars. The following morning there was no kit for me when I went in for training. I was told that I'd been suspended, I was sent home, the chairman was threatening to sue me for libel. I went away and trained on my own for a week, then got a call asking me if I fancied playing in Sweden."

Norkopping were to be Teale's next port of call, but the union would not be a happy, nor particularly long, one. "They put me up in a hotel in the middle of nowhere. It was out of the tourist season, so the place was closed except for me. Nothing about the trip made me think I wanted to move there, so I came home after four days."

Back in England, and still looking for another club, Teale found his way to Carlisle, and another short-term stay. "Martin Wilkinson was in charge, and I'd only been there for three weeks when he told me I'd be their next manager. Naturally I fancied that. Carlisle was a decent set-up even if the chairman, Michael Knighton, was totally crackers."

Carlisle were then making their annual escape from relegation to the Conference, and Teale slotted into the side well. "It was the end of the 1999-2000 season. They'd avoided going down the year before, when Jimmy Glass, the keeper who was on-loan, had scored in injury-time in the last match of the season. They were in trouble again, but I'd got a clause in my contract that said if they stayed in the Football League they'd offer me a new deal." Teale played 18 games for Carlisle, they avoided relegation yet again, and he assumed that he would be staying in the border country.

With the manager's job now vacant, and with memories of the assurances given just weeks previously, Teale could have been excused for thinking that he was about to take the first step on the managerial ladder. However, he was to receive yet another rude awakening. "I was called in to see the chairman. He'd told me the same as Martin, that I was going to get the job, then when I turned up he said, 'This is just an interview. There are others on the shortlist'. The board picked my brains for two hours then gave the job to Ian Atkins."

Teale now found himself in a position that many footballers face when coming to the end of their careers. "Carlisle offered me the deal they promised, alright. For three months, and at a third of what they were paying me already. I'd got houses in Scotland and Lancashire but I'd been living in a hotel in Carlisle. I wasn't happy about the situation so I decided to pack in full-time playing. I was 36, and time catches up with you quickly when you're that age."

Teale then returned to the place where he had first made a name for himself. "I signed for Southport, in the Conference. Mark Wright, the ex-England international, was manager with Ted McMinn, who played for Derby and Rangers, as his assistant. I was there for two years, then Mark left to take the Oxford job and I got offered the chance to be manager of Burscough, who were in the Unibond League."

Teale was player-manager of the Lancashire side for the 2002-03 season, which he remembers with obvious pride. "I played in about fifty games for them, and then came 18th May, 2003. The FA Trophy final, Burscough versus Tamworth, and it was at Villa Park as well. We were getting gates of around 180 when I arrived, and we took nearly 5,000 to the final. Tamworth outnumbered our support, but there were still around 15,000 there. We won 1-0, but the biggest thrill was to play back at Villa Park. I never thought I'd get the chance again."

Burscough did indeed win the greatest knockout honour in the non-league game, but Teale was not able to enjoy his success for long. With his usual honesty he describes how one of those situations that occur so often in non-league football came about. "My big mouth got in the way again. We had a civic reception the Tuesday after the game, at Ormskirk town hall. There was a funny atmosphere all night. Myself and the assistant manager and our wives were in one room, and everyone else was in another. No-one really spoke all night. The four of us left early, then I didn't hear a thing from the club all summer; about training, the pre-season schedule or anything at all. I got a call from one of the local press men early one Sunday morning. I told him what I was thinking at the time: that something wasn't right and that I felt there was a hidden agenda that I wasn't a part of. Then on the Tuesday I was asked to a meeting with the chairman and there was the report in the paper – two

Shaun Teale

days before it was due to be printed. I still wonder to this day if I'd been set up. The chairman went through it with me and the secretary line by line, but by then I didn't care. I said that it was what I thought at the time and it seemed as though everything was sorted.

"The secretary then said we needed to sort things out for the start of the season and that the first friendly was on July 14th. I told him that training didn't start until the day later, but they'd not bothered to find that out. Then they said that I needed to make a £1,000 a week cut in the wage bill, even though we'd just won the FA Trophy, which was worth around £75,000. I left the room disgusted, but still in a job. On the Sunday, I was receiving a memento of the Trophy win, and we were all talking about some things that needed doing at the ground. The supporters club had raised the money and Carol asked, jokingly, 'Will the money go toward the goalnets?' Next day the secretary resigns, blaming what Carol had said. There was another meeting and it was decided that I couldn't continue as manager. The chairman blamed my family."

The football career of Shaun Teale was beginning to come full circle, as he retraced his steps another time. "In December 2003 I took over as player-manager of Northwich Victoria. They were rock-bottom of the Conference, they'd sold their ground and were sharing with Witton Albion. What players we had left had nowhere to train. I took the job. I was there for a few months, then, before the last game of the season, the chairman told the players I was only the caretaker manager. I asked him if I was going to get the job permanently, because we were travelling down to Gravesend and I didn't want to go down there if I wasn't going to be manager the following season. The chairman said that I might get the job, so I told him that in that case someone else could take the team to Gravesend."

Out of football again, Teale turned to the grassroots, taking on the role of player-manager for his local side, Tarleton, in division two of the Preston & District League. In January 2005, the opportunity to get back into Pyramid-standard football arose when the manager's job came vacant at Chorley, another club in the Unibond League. "I'd been interviewed for the job two years earlier, but the budgets were lower back then. When I took over we were third from bottom, but results improved, we stayed up and I'm playing again – at 41 as well. We've got a good chairman there, Trevor Hemmings.

He won't bankroll the club but he's not trying to get something out of it either, which happens a lot in non-league."

Living in his old stamping ground between Southport and Preston with his wife, the aforementioned Carol, and their three sons, Teale has settled down nicely to the life of a former professional footballer. "I earned enough in the years I was with Tranmere to put so much into my pension that I didn't really have to work when I packed in playing. I ran a fruit and veg shop for a while but getting up at five in the morning wasn't for me."

More than ten years after leaving the Villa, Teale remains a firm favourite amongst supporters who remember with appreciation his no-nonsense approach and dedication to the game. When the club bought Dutch international defender Wilfred Bouma from PSV Eindhoven in August 2005, internet messageboards were full of debate about how the new signing would play. "He's strong, gives 100% and sometimes he'll put the ball in the stand," was the contribution of one who professed to have detailed knowledge of the Dutch game. "Sounds like Shaun Teale," was the almost immediate response from another, followed by, "That'll do."

IN THE MIDDLE

Paul Birch

Some players are remembered because they were part of a notable success, others because they gave their all in adverse circumstances. Paul Birch began his Villa career during the club's greatest achievements, but by the time he made his mark in the first team, 'adverse circumstances' had become the order of the day.

Birch was born in West Bromwich, in 1962. Signing for Villa as an apprentice straight from school, he played in the team which won the FA Youth Cup in 1980, then made his full debut as a substitute during the final stages of the European Super Cup second leg against Barcelona three years later. "An eye-opener," is his restrained way of describing how he took part in a match that saw three sendings-off, a host of bookings, and enough memorable incidents to make the game a talking point to this day. Villa, incidentally, won the game 3-0 and the tie 3-1 on aggregate.

However, this triumph was to be the last hurrah of Villa as a European force, and the next four years saw the dramatic slide that culminated in relegation at the end of the 1986-87 season. Birch had become a regular in the side but, like the rest of his colleagues, was unable to reverse the downturn once it had begun. "It didn't really have much of an effect on my career because the supporters were good to the younger players. We had the attitude of 'Let's get on with it', and the older hands helped. We knew we were all in trouble, so we just tried to battle for each other," is his memory of one of the blackest periods in the club's history.

However the players reacted, and it would not be an over-exaggeration to say that certain of them failed to share Birch's battling qualities, the team was in much better shape a few years later when the UEFA Cup draw matched Villa, the first English side to play back in Europe following the five-year ban imposed after the Heysel disaster, with Italian side Internazionale. The first leg of their tie at Villa Park saw Villa dominate from the first kick to the last in a 2-0 win. Goalscorers David Platt and Kent Nielsen grabbed the headlines, but for many people Paul Birch was the star performer as he totally outshone Lothar Mattheus, captain of the West German side who had won the previous summer's World Cup. One commentator described Birch as "never moving from Mattheus's side, kindly leading the German around Villa Park all night, for fear he might get lost." Birch for his part describes the game as, "The high spot of my career. It was a massive privilege just being on the same pitch as such great players."

However, the defeat of Inter was to prove one of the final games of Birch's Villa career. With the team's fortunes declining, a bid of £400,000 was made by Wolves manager Graham Turner, and Birch was off to Molineux in the spring of 1991. He had played 201 games for Villa, scoring 25 goals.

Many people, amongst them his manager Jo Venglos, were surprised at the speed of the move that took Birch to Wolves. He says, "I was getting on the coach to go up to Sheffield Wednesday for a reserve match when I was told to go and speak to Doug Ellis. He informed me that Wolves were interested and I was to get off to Molineux. Jo asked where I was going; he didn't know anything about it. I went over there, spoke to Graham and agreed to sign."

Turner had, of course, been Villa manager for just over two years at a time when Birch was finding his way into the side and the team's fortunes were deteriorating. However, the player had no qualms about being re-united with his former boss. "Graham had been as good as gold with me at Villa. He'd looked after the kids and I didn't have any worries about playing for him again. There wasn't any problem with the supporters, either, even though I was a Black Country lad who had played for the Villa."

Birch certainly had no problems with Villa supporters. News of his departure had been met with anger from the Villa Park crowd, who had always been appreciative of a player they saw as one of the few who had given his all over the mixed fortunes of the previous decade. Birch's final act at Villa Park was a testimonial at the start of the 1991-92 season, where the player received all the luck he deserved. He says of the occasion, "I really was in the right place at the right time. Ron Atkinson had arrived and made a load of new signings. David Platt was also there, kicking the match off and saying goodbye to the Villa supporters after his move to Bari. And thousands of Wolves fans turned up as well." The game attracted an attendance of over 19,000, the best-attended testimonial at Villa Park for many years, and those present would not have begrudged Birch a penny of the reported six-figure sum he earned.

While Turner was at Wolves, the club seemed engaged in a successful battle to avoid promotion to the Premier League. Despite being one of the best-supported teams in the first division, and certainly the wealthiest, thanks to the backing of Bahamas-based tax exile Sir Jack Hayward, it appeared as though every year they found new ways to avoid taking the place in the top flight that supporters believed to be theirs by right. Birch remains mystified as to the reason for this failure; "I haven't got a clue why we didn't go up. It would be wrong to say there was too much pressure on us, but the players certainly didn't play to their maximum ability. Graham bought some good players, but we didn't gel."

Turner was eventually replaced in March 1994, when it became clear that Wolves were destined to spend another season out of the top flight. Many thought that the board had allowed him to stay too long, but Paul disagrees. "Graham had done well. He'd saved the club from going out of business, signed Steve Bull, who must have been one of the best buys any club has made in the past twenty years, and took Wolves from the old fourth division to the second. He deserved every chance to get them up again. The players certainly thought so; there was as much respect for him in the dressing room after what proved to be his last match as there was when I arrived."

Turner's replacement was another of Birch's former managers, Graham Taylor, fresh from his disappointing reign as England boss. Again, Paul remains supportive of his old manager. "We had a lot of expectation when Graham took over. He was a highly-respected club manager, but some of the fans didn't give him a chance because of the England thing."

Taylor took Wolves to the play-offs in 1994-95, in what was to prove his only full season at Molinuex. After finishing fourth in the league programme, defeat by Bolton meant yet another season in division one, and during the summer, Taylor further alienated the Wolves supporters when their idol, Steve Bull, was linked with a move to Coventry. A bad start to the following season saw Taylor coming under renewed pressure, and he resigned as Wolves manager in November 1995.

Most observers of the Molineux scene agree that Taylor both arrived at the club and left too early, and Birch agrees. "Graham might not have been ready to take on a club job when he became Wolves manager, but he certainly shouldn't have gone when he did. The trouble was that the England thing still hung round him, and the problem with Steve Bull didn't help."

Paul certainly wasn't helped by Taylor's successor. The mere mention of the name is enough to bring a scowl to the Birch features. "Mark McGhee, say no more. There's only a handful of people in football who I haven't got on with, and he's most of them. He was arrogant, he never gave me a chance, in fact he wouldn't talk to me if we passed in a corridor. The only good thing he ever did for me was to give me a move. He didn't do too well at Wolves though, and he hasn't done a lot since, has he? His assistant, Colin Lee, did most of the coaching when they were at Wolves. Colin was okay, but McGhee... Enough said."

Birch had played 11 games on loan at Preston, scoring twice, after McGhee's arrival, and the summer of 1996 saw him making a permanent move well away from Wolves, following a Molineux career that had seen 142 league games and 15 goals.

Doncaster Rovers have never been one of the leading lights of football. At the time Birch joined them on a free transfer they were struggling in the third division, their Belle Vue home notable for being, apparently, the most valuable plot of land on which any league ground stood. However, they also had another claim to fame, or rather infamy, as a player whose career up until then had been spent in the rarified heights of the top echelons of English, even European, football, found himself caught up in one of the mysteries which occasionally bedevil the lower leagues.

Of his time at Doncaster, Birch recalls, "It was a bit of a comedown after Molineux where no expense had been spared to build one of the best grounds in the country. I noticed a difference in the facilities and the training ground, but I wasn't much bothered about that, and the supporters were marvellous. But the chairman, Ken Richardson. He seemed alright when I signed but after that, what can I say about him? Only that he was the biggest crook I've ever come across. He's the only man I've ever met in football who truly frightened people."

Villa supporters have long complained about Doug Ellis's supposed meddlings in playing matters. Compared to Richardson, though, Doug is strictly small-time. Birch continues, "He started off by sacking the manager, the old Wolves boss, Sammy Chung, the day before the season opened and bringing in Kerry Dixon, who used to play for Chelsea. He'd try to pick the team; he'd come into the dressing room before matches and try to do the team talk. Some of the younger lads were terrified of him, but I'd answer him back – so he wouldn't talk to me and he didn't want me in the side. We'd go in to training and there'd be lads there who Kerry didn't even know about. Richardson would have invited them for a trial and not told anyone."

The Doncaster chairman had already been banned from every racecourse in the country and given a suspended prison sentence for attempting to fix a horse race during in the eighties; during Birch's time he was charged with starting a fire that had destroyed the main stand at Belle Vue the previous year. Small wonder that Paul now says, "You could write a book just about what he got up to while I was there. In the end Kerry was ringing me every day to tell me whether or not I could come in for training. Things couldn't go on like that, so although I'd signed a two-year contract, I left before the end of the first season. Exeter came in for me. I drove down to meet their manager, Peter Fox, and Noel Blake, who had been in the Youth Cup-winning team with me and was now Peter's assistant, and I agreed to move down to Devon."

Despite the obvious distractions, Birch played 29 games for Doncaster during 1996-97, scoring twice; and against such a background it was little wonder that Doncaster were relegated into the Conference the season after. Richardson was later sentenced to four years imprisonment for arson.

Life in the South West was much easier, even if Paul was forced to do more travelling in order to balance professional and family commitments. "Exeter was a nice place, but it wasn't a football town.

They struggled to get more than a couple of thousand watching them and were always battling against relegation. I stayed with the club physiotherapist, Mike Chapman, for three days a week, then I'd travel back the rest of the time, home to Sutton Coldfield. My wife had just given birth to our daughter, so it was far from an ideal situation."

Noel Blake, who was player/assistant manager at Exeter, will never be fondly remembered by Villa supporters after leaving the club to join Birmingham City, but Birch retains a healthy respect for his two-time former colleague. "Noel was brilliant for us," he says. "He was very well-disciplined, which was a change from his time with Blues, and he was great to play alongside."

Unfortunately, Birch's time at Exeter came to a premature end when personal circumstances forced him to re-think his career plans. "I'd signed for two seasons again but after I'd been there just over a year my father died and I wanted to move closer to home."

Birch left Exeter at the end of the 1997-98 season, after playing 35 league games, during which he scored five goals. His career as a full-time professional at an end, he moved back to the Midlands and began playing for Halesowen Town in the Premier Division of the Dr Marten's League.

After spending time playing for a club owned by a criminal and another where home was a six-hour round trip, playing part-time at a highly-regarded club close to the area where he had lived most of his life must have come as a welcome relief to Paul: "They had a good set-up, and were getting gates of 800-odd, despite being in competition with all the other clubs in the area, although they never managed to get promoted into the Conference. Stuart Hall was manager when I first joined, then John Chambers took over. I'd been with Halesowen for two seasons and John wanted me to carry on, but by then I was 38 and I'd had enough."

The summer of 2000 saw Birch hang up his boots, although he continued to turn out for the Villa Old Stars, and take his first steps into the management side of football. "Nigel Spink was manager of Forest Green in the Conference, and asked me to be his assistant," is how he describes his first foray into coaching.

Situated in the small Gloucestershire town of Nailsworth, Forest Green were, at the time of writing, embarking upon their eighth consecutive season at the highest level of non-league football. For a club that had been playing in the junior Hellenic League just months before Birch made his debut against Barcelona, it is a story almost as impressive as Wimbledon's achievements in getting to the old first division and maintaining their top-flight status during the early years of the Premier League. Paul says of his time with Forest Green, "They didn't really have a right to be in the Conference. They weren't getting much support and had a tiny budget, but everyone worked hard and we did well. I was there for two and a bit years, first with Nigel as manager, then with Colin Addison, and we stayed in the Conference, getting to the FA Trophy final in 2001, when we lost to Canvey Island at Villa Park."

However, Birch was now finding travel once more to be a problem, and not for a reason you would normally associate with a footballer, even one who had turned his back on the full-time game. "I'd become a postman," he says candidly. "After I left Exeter I'd got fed up with sitting around doing nothing all day, so I thought I might as well do something that got me out of the house. And after all, you rarely see an unfit postman."

It's a fact of life that once someone has worked in what many would regard as a glamourous profession such as sport or showbusiness, moving back into an 'ordinary' job is somehow perceived as an admission of failure, even though it can often be better paid. When former Manchester United, Nottingham Forest and England star Neil Webb was found to be working as a postman in Reading, the news was considered worthy of the front page of the Sun. Birch, though, regarded such triviality as unimportant. "I used to go out in the morning – early in the morning – do a day's work and earn the money to pay my bills. There's no big thing about it. I'd get some digs, but nothing malicious. It helped that I was working in Erdington so most of the lads there were Villa supporters, but I didn't have any problems"

By now, Birch had left Forest Green and was working at the Birmingham City Academy for the second time. "I'd done my UEFA 'B' coaching badge after I left Exeter, and first of all I spent three months at Villa, then the Blues Academy, but I had to give that up because it was getting in the way of my full-time job. I moved to Forest Green, and when I left there, Stuart Hall, who was at Blues

Academy by then, asked me to work with him again, firstly part-time and then full-time. I started off with the under-18s and now I coach the schoolkids. I'm working towards my UEFA 'A' badge and that's my big ambition now."

Paul Birch is currently living back in West Bromwich, and has one daughter. He remains the epitome of the unsung hero, and was genuinely surprised to be told that he had made more first-team appearances for Villa than did such legends as Andy Gray and Des Bremner, while his goalscoring ratio in league games was on a par with Dennis Mortimer, although Paul would be the first to admit that his goals were often less important than those of the greatest Villa captain of modern times.

Birch has been away from Villa Park for many years, yet is still remembered in song, even though many of the Holte Enders who regularly chant his name may never have heard of his achievements. They would, though, have appreciated his efforts.

Jimmy Brown

Whatever the future may hold for Aston Villa, there are two club records that will almost certainly never be broken, and they both belong to the same man. Born in in 1953, Jimmy Brown was just 15 years and 349 days old when he made his first-team debut, in a 2-1 defeat at Bolton on 17th September 1969. Described by then-manager Tommy Docherty as "the greatest schoolboy to cross the border for years," Brown showed sufficient promise for Docherty's successor, Vic Crowe, to make him the club's youngest captain, at the age of 19, when the club returned to the second division in 1972-73.

Brown had already made his first transfer request by this time, but the young player created enough of an impression to win the supporters Terrace Trophy award for the player of the year to add to the previous season's FA Youth Cup winners medal won in the company of such future stars as John Gidman and Brian Little. However, these honours were to be the climax of Brown's career rather than the first step on the road to fame and fortune.

Brown lost first the captaincy, to Bruce Rioch, and then his first-team place. When Crowe was replaced by Ron Saunders, the Scottish midfielder failed to impress the new manager and was sold to Preston in the summer of 1975 following Villa's promotion back to the first division. He had made a total of 85 appearances for the first team, scoring one goal, and was still only 21. Contrary to popular myth, none of these games saw Jimmy appear in a half-back line with Oscar Arce and Barry Hole.

Of his time at Villa Park, Brown now says, "Maybe I was too young when I got into the first team. The managers tried to coach out of me the things I liked to do, and I couldn't go against them. It was a time when fear was starting to come into football. Everything had to be kept simple, whereas I liked to express myself. They tried to make me a different player to the one I was, and if I'd been older I could have stood up to them more than I did. I never regretted leaving Villa Park, though. Well, maybe I did. I'd have liked to stay at Villa, they were obviously on the up, but Ron Saunders was going to be around for a long time and I'd never have got much of a chance with him there."

Brown spent three years at Preston under the experienced managership of former Everton boss Harry Catterick. "A real gent," is how Brown remembers Catterick, who had taken over the reins at Preston from Bobby Charlton and retained the legendary Manchester United player's former team-mate Nobby Stiles as his assistant. "He was always immaculately dressed, always well-spoken. One day, we were playing Rotherham, and Harry took off his overcoat, removed his hat; he was wearing a pristine suit and tie. Trouble was, he used to dye his hair and that day he'd overdone the Grecian 2000. There he was, giving us the team talk and nobody could concentrate because we were all staring at this jet-black hair."

Brown enjoyed his time at Preston, at the time a mid-table club in the old third division, despite crowds that were a far cry from the thirty thousand plus who regularly watched Villa in similar circumstances. "They were a nice club, it was a good time. We only had gates of about seven thousand, but we did alright and because of Nobby's connections at Old Trafford we were able to pick up a few ex-Manchester United players, the likes of David Sadler and Micky Burns. They were good lads to have on your side."

Brown also came across a couple of players who would go on to enjoy long and illustrious careers at the game's highest levels, including a man who would go on to do great things at the Villa. "Tony Morley was just starting to make a name for himself at Deepdale. He was a tidy player, smart and sharp-looking. He never looked like a potential England player, though. Playing at a better level later on must have brought out the best in him.

"Mark Lawrenson was there as well. He couldn't get in the side. The boss put him in almost every position and he just couldn't make it. Then, as a last resort, Mark got a game as a central defender and he never looked back. He moved to Brighton, then on to Liverpool and he ended up winning every honour there was. Like Morley, he got better as he played at a higher standard."

After 64 league games, scoring four goals, Brown was given a free transfer by Preston in the summer of 1978, and took what was then the unusual decision to play in Greece. "I'd been there on holiday a few times and I liked the place. My plan was to play over there for a while, then go to end my career in America. I managed the first half of the plan, but never got round to the second."

A move to Greek first division side Ethnikos was the result, and provided Brown with some of his happiest footballing times. "It was a great set-up. They were based on the coast, in Piraeus, near Athens, and shared what was then the national stadium, the Karaiskakis, with Olympiakos. When I played for them they were getting good crowds, up to forty thousand for the big games, and we finished in the top six or seven in the league. They were a decent side, but not quite good enough to challenge the likes of Panathinaikos and Olympiakos. Greece had some superb players at the time, but there was so much politics surrounding the Greek FA that they never made much of an impact on the international scene."

Brown retains fond memories of his time in Greece. "It was tough at Ethnikos. The training was hard and we had to be careful not to over-do things due to the heat. With the sun and the beaches there was a real temptation to treat it like a holiday, but I managed to stay disciplined, which was just as well, because the supporters expected more from foreign players than from the Greek lads. I can't say a bad word about those supporters, though, because they treated us very well. During the match they were noisy and fanatical, everything you'd expect from Greek football fans, but then they'd all go home and I could walk around the town undisturbed for the rest of the week."

Brown spent over two years in Greece, before falling foul of the type of political in-fighting that is often found in clubs on the continent. "A new president took over and he wanted to bring in his own players. That often happens over there; you're doing well then, suddenly, something else is the fashion. One minute they want British players, the next it's Dutch, or German, or whatever."

Back in England, Jimmy signed for Portsmouth, then in the fourth division, for the remainder of the 1979-80 season, under the managership of Frank Burrows. "I played in almost every game for them, then on the last day of the season we had to win at Peterborough to have a chance of going up. We won 2-0 and Hull, who were above us, lost, so we got promoted. I was about 27 then, and I think I was playing the best football of my career. I had a good rapport with the supporters and things were looking good. Frank had told me that if we got promoted I'd get a new contract, then when we did go up he let me go. He said that the club was building for the future, but I had a gut feeling that he was holding something back. Maybe he just didn't like me."

Jimmy spent a short period playing for Ghent in the Belgian league ("Fantastic place, lovely people," he says of his time in Belgium), then moved back close to his roots, signing for Hibernian, under the auspices of their manager, former Birmingham City and Celtic star Bertie Auld. He helped the Edinburgh side to win promotion to the Scottish Premier League in 1980-81, playing fifteen games, before coming across a familiar story. "We went up, I got released. I was getting used to it by now. It seemed that wherever I played we'd get promoted and then I'd be let go. So basically I decided that I'd had enough of professional football and I moved back to Birmingham."

Jimmy Brown's career had now turned full circle and, like many of his contemporaries at Villa Park, he found himself drawn back to the city where he had first plied his trade. "I'd more or less grown up in Birmingham. In those days it was the sort of place you either loved or you hated, and I really loved it." Attempts to get trials with Walsall and Hereford United, then managed by Brown's former Villa team-mate Tommy Hughes, came to nothing, and his career in league football was over at the age of 28.

Brown wasn't the first footballer to give up the game only to find himself unprepared for the harsh realities of life in the outside world. "In those days players didn't have agents. In fact, we didn't have anyone to advise us at all. I didn't have a clue what wages or signing-on fees to ask for. We were left totally at the mercy of our manager."

And with unemployment rife in the West Midlands during the early eighties, it was little surprise when Jimmy Brown, with no experience of anything except playing football, found himself on the dole for two years. "I can understand why players get depressed when they give up the game. You're a footballer, you've known nothing else except training and playing, then suddenly – bang. You're not doing it anymore. The game is all you've ever worked for, and it doesn't want you, not at all. I'd have loved to have got into coaching, but to do that you need someone to give you a chance and the opportunity never came up."

Brown soon realised that the only way he would get a job in football was to give himself one, but this venture was to prove short-lived. "I started up Soccer World, which began as an after-school coaching scheme for children. We had training sessions, trips to Wembley, that sort of thing. We eventually had people coming over from around the country and Scandinavia. They'd have coaching from top pros such as Des Bremner, Nigel Spink and Gordon Cowans, play against local sides and have a look round the grounds in the area. Unfortunately it was under-funded and it went out of business. Maybe it was a bit ahead of its time."

Brown subsequently put the experience he'd gained with Soccer World to good effect by finding employment with Birmingham City Council, becoming Sports Development Officer, the role he now holds, working in Yardley and Sheldon. "We organise activities for kids, usually ones who don't belong to organised clubs, and who might not play sport at any other time."

Working with Premiership-obsessed children, though, might not always be a good thing. "I tell them that I played for the Villa, that I was the team captain, and sometimes they look at me as though I'm from another planet. You can see them thinking 'How can this ancient guy ever have been young enough to be a footballer?' Then when I go back to Glasgow some of the people I grew up with talk to me like I'm in my twenties and still playing."

Until recently, Brown turned out for the Villa Old Stars, suffering a broken leg in one charity match, and still finds time to train, whenever possible. "I play short tennis and badminton, although the distance stuff is a problem now, as the injuries I picked up playing football are starting to catch up with me. I go through periods when I'm not too healthy, then I'll start up again and train harder than when I was playing professionally."

Suffering from the effects of his playing career, Brown remains grateful to Doug Ellis for the help he was given by the oft-maligned

Villa chairman long after his time at Villa Park had ended. "I was playing tennis at the Sutton Coldfield club a few years ago when Doug noticed that I was walking stiffly. I explained that it was due to the old problem I had with my ankle and he arranged for me to get it sorted by Villa's orthopaedic surgeon, Mohammed Al-Safti, at no cost to me. I'll always be grateful to Doug for that."

When he looks round at the current crop of Villa youngsters, Brown wonders if his career might have turned out differently. "Maybe if I'd gone to a bigger team when I was a youngster, someone like Arsenal or Leeds, I might have learnt more. I wouldn't have played for the first team so early, but I would have become a better all-round player. In fact, I was all set to sign for Arsenal from school, but Tommy Docherty persuaded my parents that I'd have a better future with Villa."

He also has a warning born out of experience for the youth of today. "I was 15 and I was training with grown men in the reserve set-up. Everything was flat-out, but I didn't realise that I shouldn't have been doing that. Sprinters don't train by sprinting all the time, boxers don't spend all their training time fighting. I should have learned to pace myself. Take Charlie Aitken, for example. A magnificent athlete, but he'd train at maybe 85-90%. He'd always leave a bit for the match and so should I have done. But I was too young to know any better."

Brown's theory is backed up by former colleague Alan Deakin, whose injury-hit Villa career was coming to a close as the young Scot was starting out in the professional ranks. "Jimmy was put in the side too early," he says. "It ruined him. The same went for Walter Hazeldene. Wally played eight games for the first team when he was 16 and he hardly played after that. He'd run his legs off."

But even though Jimmy Brown's football career was curtailed, he retains his place in Aston Villa history. And it's difficult to imagine anyone taking that away from him.

Alex Cropley

It's long been said that every successful Villa side has a Scottish influence. From such legendary figures as George Ramsay and Archie Hunter in the Victorian era, to Allan Evans' role as assistant manager when Villa won their last honour to date, the Coca-Cola Cup in 1996, the Caledonian influence is firmly established at Villa Park, and anyone with more than a fleeting knowledge of the club's history will mourn the scarcity of quality footballers currently emanating from north of the border.

During the seventies Villa acquired two combative midfielders, both of whom first came to prominence whilst playing for the Scottish side, Hibernian. While Des Bremner was the more successful of the pair, winning championship and European Cup-winners medals, his compatriot Alex Cropley is arguably the better-remembered, although for no reason he would have wished.

Cropley was born in Aldershot, in 1951. The reason why such an archetypal Scottish midfielder began his life in southern England is easily explained, although there is an additional twist. "My father, John, was playing for Aldershot when I arrived on the scene. When my brother had been born two years earlier he'd moved my mother back home to make sure the new son was born in Scotland, but he didn't bother with me."

The Cropley family moved back to Edinburgh for good in 1955, with Alex leaving school at the age of 15 to work as an apprentice electrical engineer, while at the same time playing junior football for Edine Hibs. Here, his performances attracted several scouts and Alex signed professionally for the 'proper' Hibs in 1968. Cropley soon became a fixture in the Easter Road midfield and played in 118 games, scoring 27 goals, including one of the seven when his side beat Edinburgh rivals Heart of Midlothian 7-0 on New Year's Day 1973, just one of the performances which led to his being dubbed 'Scotland's George Best' and 'the White Pele' by his team's supporters.

Cropley's career was temporarily interrupted by a fractured ankle, inflicted by none other than Alex Ferguson, playing for Falkirk, and with what Cropley's then-manager Eddie Turnbull later described as a 'deliberate and cowardly' challenge. Alex did, however, gain two full Scottish caps while at Easter Road, before moving to Arsenal for £150,000 in 1974. Here he found a club under the management of Bertie Mee, who had guided them to the double in 1970-71. "He was a brilliant manager, a real gentleman," recalls Cropley, who adds, "The club was rebuilding, so results were a bit inconsistent." He also recalls a young defender by the name of David O'Leary, who was then making a name for himself in the Arsenal youth ranks. "He was a nice lad. He always looked a promising player." Cropley suffered a broken leg during his time at Highbury, which restricted his Arsenal career to just 35 appearances before a £125,000 move to Villa during the 1976-77 season.

Cropley was an immediate hit at Villa Park, playing a full part in the team's exploits of that amazing campaign, and he remembers the time fondly. "It was great. They were such an entertaining side, they played better football than the team that won the league in 1981." They could also battle as well, never more so than during the final stages of that unforgettable, marathon League Cup final against Everton. One clip of video footage from this game epitomises the tenacity that the team evinced, and the area from where much of it emerged. Villa, behind for so long in the second replay, had gone ahead with two quick goals only for Everton to draw level almost immediately. Team and supporters, all of whom had given everything, were crestfallen. Cropley can then be seen picking the ball out of the net, shaking his fist and urging one last effort from the troops around him. History recalls that Villa did, indeed, win the game with almost the last kick of extra time, and small wonder that Cropley now says, "A successful team always used to need a Scottish influence. You needed character back then, and Scots have got it in abundance."

If 76-77 had been a triumph for Alex Cropley, the following season was a nightmare. The events of 10th December 1977 are indelibly stamped on the minds of every Villa supporter who witnessed

Alex Cropley

the game against Albion. It is, if you like, the Astonian equivalent of anyone old enough to remember where they were upon hearing that President Kennedy had been shot. For reasons that have never been explained, Ronnie Allen sent out an Albion team with malice at the front of his gameplan. Leon Hickman's match report for the *Sports Argus* called their tactics "thuggish." Others used infinitely cruder terms.

Ken McNaught had already been carried off injured when Albion striker Alistair Brown challenged Cropley for a ball he had no intention of winning. Cropley recalls, "I've got a terrible memory, but I remember everything about that tackle as though it was yesterday. I've got to the ball, pushed it forward and he's come in, straight-legged, right over the top and then, snap – I'm on the floor screaming 'My leg!!!' I'm there and I'm holding my leg together. I look up and Andy Gray's holding Brown over the dug-out. If he'd known my leg had gone, God knows what Andy would have done. My girlfriend of the time was in the crowd and at half-time Jimmy Hill came over to her, he was working for the BBC at the match, and he just shrugged his shoulders. There was nothing more he could say."

If Gray was unaware of the extent of his colleague's injury, he must have been the only one inside Villa Park who remained in ignorance, for the sound of Cropley's leg breaking had echoed around Villa Park. Anyone who thinks that this is an exaggeration and such a noise could never be heard over the tumult of a packed football ground simply wasn't there. It remains, to this day, one of the most vivid memories amongst Villa followers of the period, etched on the memories of all who witnessed it. Cropley, naturally, remains angry about the entire affair. "It was always reckoned that Villa against Blues was the big local derby, but the Albion was just as bad. They really had it in for us. The previous season, Len Cantello had tackled Ray Graydon and Ray was never the same again." And to this day, Alex retains an understandable loathing of the man who finished his top-flight career. "A couple of years ago I was on holiday in Portugal and I got talking to this lad who was a Baggies supporter. I asked him about Ally Brown and he said that he saw him occasionally. I was so close to asking him, 'Tell the bastard that you've met Alex Cropley'."

Cropley's career at the top was, indeed, more or less over. Problems with his leg meant he was in plaster for seven months, and although he made a full recovery, this unluckiest of players added a mere handful of appearances to his Villa record during the 1979-80 season before breaking an ankle. Again, recovery was slow but full, although by this time a new generation of Villa players had taken his place and, with the team doing so well, Cropley was unable to get back into the first team. A period on loan at Newcastle failed to kick-start his career, with just three league games started. "When I got there they were top of the second division. They'd lost the Saturday before, and that was the beginning of their slide. I was there for a month and I think they only won once in that time."

Cropley's time at Newcastle had seen him link up with future Villa legend Peter Withe who, despite having won the first division title with Nottingham Forest a few years previous, was still a long way off the player he was to become at Villa. He did, though, create enough of an impression for Alex to remember them playing together. "Even then Peter was the dominating force in the team. Everything had to go through him and he seemed suited to the level where he was playing. I'll give him his due, though, a couple of years later he'd transformed himself. I'd still prefer Andy Gray, but Peter had gone from second division journeyman to international, and good luck to him for that. That was where Ron Saunders excelled; he always replaced players with others who were like them. Frank Carrodus went, and Des Bremner took his place. Chris Nicholl was sold, Ken McNaught was signed. Andy left, Peter came in."

Cropley left Villa Park for good at the end of the 1980-81 season, a time when everyone else at the club was celebrating championship success. He had played 82 games, scoring seven goals, and says of the period leading up to his departure, "Ron Saunders told me he couldn't guarantee me a first team place, which was fair enough. Gordon Cowans was doing well and there were younger lads than me in the reserves, players such as Gary Shelton and Mark Walters. I got talking to Bruce Rioch, who by coincidence had also been born in Aldershot and had Scots parents. He was playing in America and persuaded me to sign for Toronto Blizzard, so I moved out there for the summer of 1981. It was a fabulous place to live; I had a great time. The football was easy because there were a lot of players who had the attitude that it was just a holiday for them, whereas I had a lot to prove and I was always keen in every game I played, whatever the circumstances. That was why I was a bad player in testimonials – I tended to treat them too seriously."

Expatriate Villa supporter Norm Crandles saw several of Cropley's appearances for Blizzard, and bears out Alex's description of himself. "He never stopped running, and that was no mean feat with the temperatures they played in. Alex was a hungry type of player, always seemed to be around the ball."

Cropley came back from a summer in Toronto to play for Portsmouth, then in the third division under manager Frank Burrows. He recalls, "It was a difficult time. I'd signed a contract with them but it might as well have been written in pencil. The manager said he wanted me to sit in midfield and spray the ball round, but as everyone knows, that doesn't work in the third division. You have to battle for everything and there's a lot of lumping the ball forward. I'd lost much of my enthusiasm for the game, as well. I'd always loved playing, but after you leave Villa, well, you only realise just what a great club they are after you've gone They were a big club, but they were still just like a family, there was a great atmosphere about the place."

Cropley played 10 times for Portsmouth in the 1981-82 season, scoring twice, but by then his enthusiasm for football had all but died. "I'd had a couple of injuries, and the ankle problem still hadn't cleared up. All the problems I'd had were catching up with me. I spoke to Bobby Campbell, who was the club's coach, and he said that both he and Frank Burrows agreed that I should retire. I went along with them."

However, the terms of Cropley's retirement soon led to disagreement. "We agreed a package, then they sent me a letter saying that I would only receive eleven weeks' money. I complained, the PFA backed me, and the affair went to a tribunal that took place at the Metropole Hotel, near the NEC. It was a bit of a farce, although it went well for me. Portsmouth ended up giving me a testimonial, and Villa's European Cup-winning side turned out, but it was at a time pre-season when Portsmouth had about seven games in a fortnight so there wasn't much of a crowd."

Cropley spent some time after his retirement living in Sutton Coldfield, pondering the eternal question of what a former footballer does after leaving the game. "I thought I might have a crack at getting into coaching. The youth team job had just come up at Villa because Keith Leonard had joined Ron Saunders at Blues, so I applied for that. Tony Barton was very fair with me, but he said that Brian Little, who had also just had to retire from playing, was getting the job. Fair play to Brian, he did well at it."

Little did, indeed, use his appointment as youth team coach at Villa Park as the springboard for a successful managerial career, but for Cropley, this was yet another setback. "I thought I'd got the right attitude to be a coach, but I wasn't qualified. There was also a bit of a problem because I thought I didn't have a great reputation within the game. It had been a few years since I'd been playing regularly in the first division, so I was a bit of a forgotten man."

Cropley and his family moved back to Edinburgh, where he opened a bar, unsurprisingly named Cropley's. "It did alright for a few years, then the recession started to bite and business dropped throughout the pub trade. I was made a good offer for the place so I sold up round about 1986. I was in insurance for a bit, but that just didn't suit me. It was like being back at school, and I never enjoyed that very much back when I was a child, so being around 36 by now, I was never going to do very well. I thought then that I'd give taxi driving a try. I passed my exams, got a cab and here I am. I've been doing it for about 16years and I still enjoy it."

He may enjoy his work, and it would be a foolhardy passenger who gave Alex Cropley any problems, but I've yet to be convinced of the merits of his home city. Every time I've visited Edinburgh the weather has been lousy and the day that I met Alex was no different. Walking down Princes Street, I suffered rain, hail, sleet and snow within the course of ten minutes and then, after eventually drying out in one of the many coffee shops that seem to be multiplying as rapidly in Edinburgh as everywhere else in Britain, I was promptly drenched by a van driver who sailed through a puddle without worrying about the consequences of saturating a poor Sassenach 300 miles from his nearest dry clothing. Indeed, had he known I was an Englishman, he would doubtless have claimed bonus points.

Cropley may have severed his links with the game, but he still enjoys watching Hibs, even if he sometimes fails to attract the respect his talent and service to the club where he performed with such distinction deserves. "I get recognised from time to time when I'm working," he says, although he admits, "The people who saw me play are getting thin on the ground these days." He still, however, attends games at Easter Road, work commitments permitting, and has strong views on the way the Scottish game is progressing. "Football in Scotland isn't much good now," he believes. "There are too many bodies involved. The Scottish Premier League, the Scottish League, the SFA. They should get together to sort it all out. There's not enough money in the game up here, and television isn't doing it any great favours. It's easy to support the Old Firm or one of the top teams in England by watching television and that's what a lot of the young children getting into football do."

However, should a new Scottish hero emerge, he may well have a familiar name. One of Cropley's sons (he is married, with two sons and two daughters) is now playing for Hibs under-17s despite still being at school. There may still be a chance that a third generation of Cropleys will make the professional grade. His father, though, has a typically no-nonsense warning. "I've told him, if I ever see him kissing the badge on his shirt I'll run on the pitch and kick his backside. I've no time for that kind of nonsense." Nonsense and Alex Cropley never were on speaking terms.

Alan Deakin

It was the opening day of the 2004-05 season. Villa had beaten Southampton 2-0 at home – a none-too convincing performance against a side who would subsequently be relegated and almost the only thing of note throughout the game was a stunning display from debutant Carlton Cole, on loan from Chelsea. Few people took much notice of the jovial, white-haired man as they filed out of the North Stand once the final whistle blew, but if they had, they would have heard him commenting ruefully on the lack of bite in the Villa midfield.

Some would doubtless have thought him a typical member of the older generation, forever complaining that things were much better in his day. Some would have agreed with his analysis of the game. And others, recognising a semi-familiar face from years gone by, would have realised that here was a man who knew a thing or two about quality midfield players, because, at his peak, he'd been one of the best there was.

Alan Deakin was one of that crop of youngsters who became known as the Mercer Minors as they briefly lit up the Villa Park scene during the early sixties, providing a glimmer of hope amidst years of decline. Indeed, there are many learned judges who would consider him to have been the best of the lot.

Born in Walsall, in 1941, Alan arrived at Villa Park as a 15 year old, straight from school. Eric Houghton was manager at the time, but Alan became a first-team regular under Eric's successor, Joe Mercer. In all, he made 269 appearances for the club, scoring nine goals. He played most of these games as a wing-half and almost all were prior to an injury in 1966 which saw one of the most promising Villa careers of the day severely disrupted, shortly after Deakin had been made team captain. He recalls, "We were playing Fulham and I went into a tackle with Graham Leggatt, who later became a coach with the Villa. He ended up with eight stitches in his ankle, but I broke my leg and I was never the same again. I don't think I played more than twenty games for the first team after that."

Not only was Deakin's Villa career virtually over, but the incident also terminated what had been up until then a promising progression through the England ranks. "I made six appearances for the England under-23 team, and I captained them on a couple of occasions. I'd got into the England 'B' and the Football League representative squads, although I'd had to pull out through injury both times, and I'd been called into the full England squad, when Walter Winterbottom was manager. I was also on the bench for Young England against Old England at Stamford Bridge in 1965, but breaking my leg was the end of my international hopes."

However, Deakin concedes that, injury or no, he stood little chance of breaking into the full England set-up on their way to the World Cup finals of 1966. "At that time there seemed to be a definite London bias. There were some great players in the Midlands – Harry Burrows and John Sleeuwenhoek at Villa, Ron Flowers and Peter Broadbent at Wolves, players like that, but they never got a look-in. It got better later on, but it was still harder to be dropped from the England squad than to be selected for it in the first place."

As Villa, the undisputed giant of Victorian football, struggled with the realities of a rapidly-changing sixties world, relegation from the top flight in 1967 confirming that they were no longer one of the great names of English football, so Alan Deakin was condemned to an equally fruitless struggle to maintain a top-level career. A succession of injuries, most notably knee problems, restricted his first-team appearances as Villa slid inexorably towards the third division. "I'd started out as a wing-half and as football developed, I became a midfielder. Then, when that got a bit too much for my legs, I dropped back into the centre of defence."

The arrival of Tommy Docherty in 1968 threatened briefly to halt the team's slide, but Deakin's days at Villa Park were numbered. "I only played one game under Docherty. Some of the players didn't get on with him; but, speak as you find, I liked him and he was good to me."

By now, though, Deakin realised that his Aston Villa career was coming to an end and moved on a free transfer to Walsall, then occupying what is generally regarded as their natural position in the grand footballing scheme of things, mid-table in the old third division. Here, Alan linked up with former Villa trainer Bill Moore, who had worked with Eric Houghton to guide Villa to FA Cup final success in 1957, when the young Deakin had been on the Villa Park ground staff. He recalls, "Bill was a great bloke, but he was on his second stint as Walsall manager and, as is often the case, he shouldn't have gone back."

Deakin spent three seasons at Walsall, playing 53 games, and one of his fondest memories of his time at Fellows Park remains the four league fixtures with Villa, games which live in the hearts of all the Saddlers fans who witnessed them. Walsall club historian Geoff Allman, a regular at Fellows Park at the time, recalls, "Alan's best game for us was the 3-0 victory at home to Villa in 1970. He'd slowed down a bit by then, and he couldn't really perform for ninety minutes, but he was a keen tackler and he used the ball well."

Deakin says of the games he played against his old club, "Villa couldn't beat us in the two seasons they were in the third. But to be fair, in those days the visiting club used to be paid a share of the gate receipts and the money Walsall earned from the big crowds at Villa Park helped keep them in business." Indeed, Walsall's defensive performance in the following season's goal-less draw at Villa Park moved one commentator to write, "All Walsall came for was the gate money."

Money was, indeed, tight at Fellows Park, which was just one of the problems Deakin faced as he adjusted to life at what has always been the area's smallest, and often friendliest, club. "They were good times at Walsall. Everyone had to pitch in to keep the club going and although I got on fine with the supporters and everyone else at the club, I never really had the same feeling that I had at the Villa. At least we always got paid, though. I don't doubt that it was a struggle sometimes, but we got our wages every week."

Walsall's finances were helped not only by the temporary presence of Villa in the same division, but also by a run to the fourth round of the FA Cup in 1972. "We beat Bournemouth, when they had Ted McDougall and Phil Boyer in the side and John Bond was their manager. Then we played up at Everton and got beat 2-1 in front of about forty thousand."

Walsall's brightest hope at the time was forward Bernie Wright, and his performances during that cup run persuaded Everton to pay £20,000 for a player whose stay at Goodison was as brief as it was controversial. "Bernie was a bit of a rough diamond, to put it mildly. I warned him when he left that Everton was a great opportunity but he had to watch his step up in Liverpool. I don't think he took much notice, though. I heard that almost as soon as he arrived up there he got on the wrong side of Howard Kendall, and that was never going to help him." And so it proved, with Wright lasting less than twelve months at Everton before his contract was cancelled and he returned to Walsall in January 1973. By now, though, Alan Deakin had left the club and had, in fact, given up professional football altogether.

Deakin took his coaching badges while at the Villa, but was never really interested in exploring this side of the game. "I didn't give it much thought. It wasn't really the done thing then to move straight into coaching or management, although when I see how much the managers get paid now, especially when they get such big pay-offs for failing and getting the sack, I wouldn't mind having a go. It's incredible – where else would you get so rich for doing a bad job?"

Deakin did, though, experience a brief taste of life as a coach when injury forced him out of Villa's tour of the USA in the summer of 1969. "Tommy Docherty asked me to take the youth team over to Amsterdam to play in the Blau-Wit tournament." It was at this time that he first really noticed a youngster from the emergent Villa youth set-up named Brian Little. "You could tell he was going to be special. Even at 15 there was something about him."

But this was to be the closest Deakin ever got to management, and the harsh realities of life outside football soon came calling once he left Walsall. Like many of his contemporaries, Alan Deakin had always looked to the future. "We all knew that we'd have to get a proper job when we packed in playing. There were only a handful of players – George Best, Bobby Charlton, people like that – who earned so much that they could save enough to live on after they'd retired. Footballers were better paid than most people, but we always said that was because the life was so short and uncertain. It's not like now, with players on four-year contracts. No other business has got anything like it."

Indeed, it's doubtful that any retiring Premiership player will undergo the career progression that Deakin embarked upon once he left the professional game. "Once I knew I was leaving Walsall I applied to join a twelve-month Government training scheme and qualified as a welder. I was lucky in that the course finished on the Friday and I got a job starting on the following Tuesday. I worked from then on until I had to give up – never had a day out of work.

Some of the bad luck that Deakin had suffered with injuries did, though, continue to dog him, or, rather, his employers. "I was with Metro Camell, the bus makers, for fourteen years, then they closed down. I moved to Gimwell Engineering, on Witton Island, right next to Villa Park. I worked there for three years, before they closed. Finally I moved to Scamell Engineering, in the city centre. I was there for five years before I had to give up work through ill-health when I was 57, and they closed down after I left."

Once retiring from full-time football, Deakin had found himself unable to give up the game completely. "I was with Tamworth, in the Southern League, for three seasons. I was happy there; we had some good players, but there was a bit of money trouble there and we had to put a lot of kids in the side. My knees were holding up better by that time than they had for years, and I was enjoying my football again."

Originally intending to give up the game at this point, Deakin found the lure of playing – and helping out an old claret and blue colleague into the bargain – too strong. "John Sleeuwenhoek was manager of Pelsall Villa, who were in the West Midlands League, and he asked me if I'd turn out for them as a favour to him. I didn't fancy it, but John persuaded me and in the end I had a couple of seasons there. It was a nice place to play, they were lovely people and they had a good set-up, but when John stepped down as manager in 1976, I left as well."

Now retired, Alan Deakin lives in Aldridge, and, like many an old Villan, retains links with the club via the Former Players Association. "I played for the Old Stars from when I left Tamworth up until the mid-nineties, and they look after us well. The same goes for the PFA. They get some stick, but when I needed a knee operation a few years ago they covered the bill, just as they paid for an electric wheelchair for Jimmy Dugdale."

Divorced ("It just didn't work out. We're still friends – there's no point in not getting on"), with two sons, one of whom lives in Indonesia and fortunately escaped the Tsunami disaster which befell the country at Christmas 2004, Alan Deakin remains philosophical about his football career. "I had some great years," he says. "I wouldn't have changed a thing."

And Villa finished the 2004-05 season in mid-table, missing out on UEFA Cup qualification thanks in part to a slump in form towards the end of the season. Many supporters blamed this on a lack of inspiration from midfield. If they'd been in the North Stand when the season began, they'd have known what was coming all along.

Ian Hamilton

Mention Ian Hamilton to most Villa supporters and there's a good chance they wouldn't know who you were talking about. Say Chico Hamilton and, regardless of the team they support, fans from the seventies will instantly recognise the name. Never mind that he left English football at the comparatively early age of 28, or that most of his playing career was spent in the lower divisions, Chico Hamilton remains the epitome of the carefree, mercurial seventies footballer, and much of that reputation is down to the nickname he acquired while still a schoolboy in the South London suburb of Streatham.

"I was training with Chelsea twice a week, and I suppose I was a bit of a cheeky so and so. Someone called me Cheeky, it got altered to Chico, and the name stuck. My family and friends call me Ian, but everyone else knows me as Chico. If someone shouts 'Ian', I usually wonder who they're talking to. I can't complain, though. It's been good to me; everyone remembers me because of it."

Born in 1950, Chico left school to join Chelsea as an apprentice, under the management of Tommy Docherty, and was considered promising enough to make his first-team debut at 16. He made an immediate impact, scoring in a 1-1 draw with Spurs whose scorer that day was none other than the legendary Jimmy Greaves.

Despite such a promising start, Hamilton's career at Stamford Bridge was limited to just five appearances, in which he scored two goals, and by September 1968 he was on his way to fourth division Southend for a fee of £5,000. Hamilton did well in his time at Roots Hall, scoring 11 goals in 36 games, and once more attracted the attention of Tommy Docherty, by now attempting to rebuild Villa overnight. A £40,000 price was agreed, and Hamilton promptly arrived at Villa in the summer of 1969, to join what would prove a vain attempt to keep the club out of the third division.

He says of Docherty, and his managerial successor Vic Crowe, "Tommy came in and straight away it seemed as though the dressing room was split. You were either with the Doc or against him, it was rare that you heard anyone at Villa Park say they weren't bothered about him. It was love or hate. Then Vic came in and he did a great job in bringing us all together. He and his assistant, Ron Wylie, were a lot more laid back. They knew that we'd be out at night during the week, but they let us have a lot more freedom than we'd had when Tommy was in charge. Then again, there was less pressure on them because by then we were getting the results."

Villa certainly got results during the initial stages of Crowe's reign, being promoted to the second division in 1971-72 with a record points total, but, as his revival ran out of steam, Crowe was sacked and replaced for the 1974-75 season by Ron Saunders, who gained immediate success. Hamilton recalls the time with fondness: "We must have lost a game after Christmas of that year, but I can't remember one. We couldn't stop scoring, we were beating everyone, but we were never complacent."

Hamilton ended the season with 14 goals, one of four Villa players who netted ten or more as the team scored over a hundred times on their way back to the first division, with the League Cup thrown in for good measure. Promotion was gained, and Hamilton began the new season with Villa back in the top flight. Unfortunately for the player, Ron Saunders felt that the flamboyant style that had proved so successful the previous season needed to be changed, so Chico was eased out of the side by the end of 1975-76. Sheffield United made a £50,000 offer for his services, and Chico Hamilton found his Villa career over in the summer of 1976, after 232 games, during which he had scored 48 goals.

He was soon to learn that moving to a side newly relegated to the second division was the wrong decision. "I shouldn't have gone there. Sheffield's a fabulous place, but the team were poor and things were on the slide. Jimmy Sirrell was manager. He signed Jimmy Johnstone, who'd been great for Celtic when they won the European Cup, but that had been nine years earlier. The club put Johnstone in a top hotel as well. That's not too clever for a heavy drinker. United were paying for everything on his bill and Jimmy took full advantage – including the Rolls-Royce he drove round in."

Chico spent two seasons at Bramall Lane, and although he maintained a respectable goalscoring record of hitting the net 13 times in 60 games, found himself more than willing to leave England when the opportunity arose during the summer of 1978 to play in North America. "Freddie Goodwin, who I knew from when he was manager of the Blues, was in management in the States, and he got me to sign for Minnesota Kicks. I had a fabulous time over there. We were right up on the Canadian border, so it was cold – minus 58 degrees once and we had 66 days in a row below zero at one point, but it was a fantastic place. My family were living with me, the football was good and we were getting 32,000 watching us.

"Everything about Minnesota was great. I played against New York Cosmos in the play-offs, and Pele signed a photo for me, 'To Chico', even though I don't think he spoke much English back then. We used to do a lot of coaching in the schools as well, although a lot of the kids didn't know what 'soccer' was."

Hamilton was in good company as Kicks engaged the services of such notables of the English game as Charlie George and Steve Heighway in an attempt to compete with their big city rivals. For their part, the new team-mates certainly made the most of a lifestyle that was completely at odds with the grim times back home, and thoroughly enjoyed the atmosphere in which they found themselves caught up. "We'd go on trips along the river, sitting in these enormous truck tyres full of beer and food. I doubt Premiership players could get away with the sort of adventures we had, but we were a long way from home, and it was great for getting to know the rest of the team. We were away for so long that we needed things like that to make it all bearable."

Hamilton spent four years in Minnesota before falling victim to what was to become a familiar tale as the always-fragile bubble that was the North American Soccer League began to burst. "This guy named Ralph Sweets, who'd been a director of Notts County when Jack Dunnett was their chairman, took over the Kicks. Suddenly there was money being spent everywhere, and we couldn't see where it was coming from. Then without any warning, after a year, the club went bust. I don't know why, but I've got my suspicions. Sweets left, although I wouldn't say he was involved in anything dodgy, and we found ourselves without wages. The cars the players were driving were taken back, and we were in real financial trouble. We even had to hold garage sales to raise some money."

While many of the Englishmen who played in the NASL either did so only during our close-season, or moved back home when the great American adventure started to turn sour as the eighties began, Chico decided to stay and seek another club. Somewhat predictably, bearing in mind the Hamilton persona, he headed for California, and signed for the San Jose Earthquakes in the summer of 1981. "Another great place," is his opinion of life on the West Coast. "The climate was fabulous this time, as well."

Hamilton spent a year in California before deciding to return to England. He admits, though, that his was hardly the return of the prodigal. There was no divine right to employment for a player whose career in the Football League was becoming a fast-fading memory, particularly during the early eighties recession which hit especially hard in Chico's adopted homeland of South Yorkshire. "Things were tough for a bit. I had problems with my achilles, which meant that I was waking up in pain and I could hardly walk for a couple of years, so any kind of work within football was out of the question for a long while."

Chico's natural resilience, though, meant that he was always liable to bounce back. And so it proved, in the unlikely surroundings of Rotherham United's unimposing Millmoor ground. "I got a job working for Football in the Community with local youngsters. That was great at first; when it started off it was government-funded and the kids didn't have to pay. Then the emphasis gradually changed so that we had to generate the funds ourselves and we had to start charging a lot of those who were attending our courses. There's a lot of deprived areas around there, and it was the kids from these places who stopped coming, even though they were the ones who needed the scheme the most.

"I worked at the club for five years, then I thought it was time for a change. I'm not being critical of Rotherham, because they didn't have the money to improve the way their community schemes were being run, but it was hardly the best surroundings to work in. There was a great atmosphere amongst the people I was working with, but we couldn't get on with the work we'd liked to have done because the money wasn't there."

Chico moved back to working in Sheffield in 1993, although he has lived in the city since his initial return from America. "I got a job with the Sheffield University Play Scheme, originally as a playworker and now as co-ordinator. The scheme started off for the benefit of staff and students at the university, so that their children had somewhere they could be dropped off and looked after during the holidays, and now it's been extended to cover the public."

Chico had been returning to America intermittently between 1992 and 1995, to coach youngsters in Manassas, Virginia. "By now they'd got into football over there, and we could see the progress they'd made, especially in the women's game. I'd got my FA coaching badges while I was at Rotherham, but I never really used them apart from when I was in the States. I didn't fancy being a coach full-time."

Describing himself, typically, as "Twice married, one and a half times divorced," and with two step-children and a son, Hamilton still lives in Sheffield, occasionally attending matches at Bramall Lane, but more often than not confining his football watching to television. We got together the day after United's unlucky defeat on penalties in the fifth round of the 2004-05 FA Cup to eventual winners Arsenal. "I saw the game on TV, but I wasn't all that bothered about it," was his throwaway comment about the previous night's proceedings.

In addition to working at the university, Chico also works for a private after-school club, again with the job title of co-ordinator. The Hamilton smile flashes as he says, "I seem to do a lot of co-ordinating."

It's difficult to imagine footballers, most of whom have been isolated from the perils of the real world from an early age, having the ability to look after groups of energetic children, particularly when they involve the kind of story of which most of us, luckily, have no experience. Hamilton, though, appears in his element as he discusses the job. "We sort out day trips, and take them for camping holidays. It's tough. We have kids from deprived backgrounds that you wouldn't believe, and it can sometimes be very difficult to understand what drives them to behave as they do. I found one young lad banging his head against the wall recently. I can only imagine what he's gone through that makes him do that."

And on a lighter note, there's the age-old problem of convincing his charges that he, too, was a professional footballer, playing at the grounds they know only from television and earning a living from the kind of life they imagine is the exclusive preserve of the Gods. "They can't believe I played football for Villa and Chelsea," Chico says. "I have to take my old photos in to prove to them that I used to be a footballer."

Kevin Richardson

Kevin Richardson will always play a significant part in the history of Aston Villa, and not only as captain of the memorable Coca-Cola Cup-winning team that defeated Manchester United in 1994. He also skippered the side during the previous season, when a little more luck, and possibly self-belief, would have given Villa the inaugural Premier League title, and with it Kevin would have enjoyed the unique honour of winning the championship with three different clubs.

Had Villa won that initial Premiership crown, condemning Manchester United to what was then another year without the title they would go on to consider theirs by right, the history of English football over the next decade might have been completely different. Villa may not have attracted as many gloryhunters as has United, but equally the Old Trafford club might never have gone on to become such a dominant force in those pre-Abramovitch days.

Born in Newcastle in 1962, Kevin joined Everton straight from school, and gradually made his way through the Goodison Park ranks, finally establishing himself in the first-team squad during the 1983-84 season, when his side played Villa in what was to be a fateful League Cup semi-final.

Everton manager Howard Kendall, who had born the brunt of much criticism earlier in the season, was seemingly improving matters, while Tony Barton was attempting to re-build the European Cup-winning side of two seasons earlier. With Everton two up in the first leg at Goodison, Kevin got away with a blatant handball on the goal-line. There were no further goals in the game. Villa won the return leg 1-0, but Everton went on to the final, then won the FA Cup that season, the Cup-Winners Cup the following year and the championship twice in three seasons, while Villa were relegated during the same period.

Had Villa won the tie, things may have been different, and Richardson well remembers the time. "I'd broken my wrist in the league game a few weeks earlier, when Steve McMahon had pulled me down and I'd fallen awkwardly. I was still wearing a covering over it, and yes, you could see the mark where the ball hit it.

"We'd been playing badly, and Howard Kendall's job was under threat. Then we beat Oxford in the quarter-final, when Adrian Heath got a late equaliser. We won the replay, and it all went on from there. It was the same players, doing the same things, but suddenly we were on fire."

Kevin played 109 league games for Everton, scoring 14 goals, before leaving in the summer of 1986 to join Watford, then managed by Graham Taylor. As seems to be obligatory for players who came into contact with Taylor, Richardson speaks highly of the man who was then in what would prove to be his final season at Vicarage Road before joining Villa. "A lovely man. I have loads of respect for him, but he wanted to play things his way. I'd been brought up to play football and I managed to adapt to Graham's style, but at the end of the season he left to join Villa. Dave Bassett took his place and things got a bit difficult, so I moved again."

After just 39 games for Watford, scoring two goals, Kevin signed for Arsenal, the fee being a reported £400,000. Once more he found himself in the right place at the right time, joining a side that George Graham was putting together which would mount a challenge for the title. "George was another great manager. He got some stick for the way we played, but we were able to play as the situation suited. We could pass it round or we could hit long balls up to Alan Smith."

Richardson played in the final game of the 1988-89 season, at Anfield. Arsenal, second to Liverpool in the table, had to win by two clear goals to take the title and promptly did so, the decisive goal coming from Michael Thomas with just seconds remaining. It was the most dramatic finale in league history, as Kevin recalls. "Looking back, the drama was absolutely frightening. George said the game would unfold with a tense, goal-less first half, then we'd nick a goal after the break and go on to win late on, and that's what happened. You couldn't write a better script, and it was even better for me with being a former Everton player."

Richardson left Arsenal during the following summer, after 95 games and five goals, a fee of £750,000 taking him to Spain, where he played for Basque side, Real Sociedad. "I enjoyed myself over there. San Sebastian, where Real play, is a beautiful city on the coast, but, unfortunately, while I was there they had the worst winter they've ever had, so we didn't exactly see much of the beach."

After a year and 37 games in La Liga, Richardson returned to join Ron Atkinson's revolution at Villa Park, his £400,000 price tag being one of the smaller fees Ron paid during the summer of 1991, and was made captain in place of the Italy-bound David Platt. "A tremendous player," was how Atkinson later described his skipper. "We were bringing Dalian (Atkinson) back and they offered us Kevin as well. He was a bonus."

Kevin himself says, "Ron knew all about me, and Andy Gray, who was his assistant and I'd played with at Everton, persevered in signing me. Sociedad had got three English players: me, Dalian and John Aldridge, and they had to get rid of us all because they hadn't qualified for Europe. The manager had been sacked and John Toshack was in charge, although he couldn't be officially named manager because of some Spanish league regulation, so he was keeping in touch via the coaches. I knew what was going on, and I fancied a move back home."

Atkinson's initial season was one of re-building, and was followed by a memorable 1992-93. Kevin recalls with obvious pride and nostalgia what was to become one of the best-loved Villa sides of recent memory. "Ron buys footballers. We looked after the ball, and we could play a bit as well. Everyone complemented each other – even in defence we looked stylish. Steve Staunton was out on the left, Paul McGrath and Shaun Teale did their bit.

"Ron used to give us one instruction – go out and enjoy yourself. Players nowadays are told what to do, they have their job and there aren't many who express themselves, they keep to the book. You should be able to assess the situation, and Ron let us do that. He'd say what he wanted us to do, but he also instilled that confidence which made you feel you could try something a bit different."

The following season was a disappointing one in the league, but had its compensations in the form of a memorable, and ultimately successful, League Cup campaign that kicked-off with a comfortable two-legged win over Blues, notable for Paul Tait's assault on Kevin at Villa Park. "I'd gone in to tackle him, and he didn't like the challenge. He came at me, I put my arms up and he pushed me over. I was standing by the wall of the stand and I went into the crowd, luckily into the arms of a good-looking young lady. Tait was sent off, we won."

As the cup run progressed, Villa seemed to be making almost inexorable progress toward Wembley. "The big clubs kept getting knocked out and we were wondering 'Who else is left that could beat us?' But of course, even the smaller clubs can be hard to beat."

Especially if their name is Tranmere. "That one was too close for my liking. They played above themselves, pushed us all the way and they could have put the game beyond us up there."

But they didn't, and with the tie finishing 4-4 on aggregate, it was down to the penalties that have entered Villa Park folklore and remain imprinted on the Richardson memory. "I'm useless at penalties and I always was. I'd missed one in the cup the year before against Wimbledon, so there was no way I was taking one of the first five. Then after that, I think it was four apiece; we were looking for someone to take the next one. Andy Townsend was injured; it wouldn't have been fair on a couple of the younger lads, and Tony Daley and Ray Houghton were looking the other way. There was a gap of a few seconds where nobody wanted to take number six and it looked bad so I thought 'Bollocks to this, I'll have a go'. I stepped up, determined to blast the ball into the back of the net, and thank God the glass in the North Stand executive boxes is tough. We were in trouble then, but Bossie saved one. Tony Daley, ironically, took one of the best penalties of the lot, then Bos saved another. I made sure I took him a bottle of champagne the next day to say thanks. He certainly helped me that afternoon."

Villa, of course, won the final, with Kevin making his mark as one of the handful of Villa captains to have lifted a trophy at Wembley. There was also the added bonus at the end of the season of an England cap when he featured in Terry Venables' side against Greece.

Winning the League Cup, though, had disguised a worrying drop in Premiership form from the highs of the previous season, and this was to have serious consequences in 1994-95, which had begun with

Kevin Richardson 113

Ron already coming under fire for the lengthy period of time he'd spent working in the media during the World Cup finals in the USA. His captain, however, remains a staunch defender of the then-Villa manager. "Ron would have been looking at players all the time he was over there. It was hard to compete with the big clubs for new signings, but I'm sure Ron was watching proceedings with great interest. If he failed to sign a player, though, he was hardly likely to admit it."

The start of the season saw a seemingly regular script, in which Villa would dominate games but fail to score, inevitably losing to a late goal. Though the performances were good, and Atkinson's stock with the fans equally high, it was the results that had taken Villa into the relegation places which saw Ron's time at Villa Park draw to a close with a farcical press announcement, made to the waiting press by a visibly-nervous commercial manager, Abdul Rashid, as Villa Park locked its gates to the world. Richardson simply says of the manager's dismissal, "We were battering teams but not scoring goals. That's what cost him his job."

The arrival of Brian Little led, ultimately, to a turnaround in the team's fortunes and another League Cup win, By this time, though, Kevin Richardson had moved on, both his role in the centre of midfield and the captaincy handed to Andy Townsend, signed by Atkinson but given a new lease of life by his successor. "Andy hadn't done too well at first because he'd been played wide, and although he had good technique, he lacked a bit of pace. Brian was a nice fella, but I wasn't his type of player so I was off."

Richardson left Villa Park in 1995, after 171 games, most of them as captain, during which time he scored 16 goals. He linked up again with Ron Atkinson at Coventry for a fee of £300,000. At this time, City were trying to escape the tag of perennial relegation strugglers. "There was a high turnover of players, there was a lot of money being spent, but the best of the lot didn't cost him anything. Gordon Strachan arrived, and what a player he was. His fitness levels were unbelievable – he played until he was 39, and he could have carried on even then. In 1997 when we had to win at Spurs on the last day of the season to stay up, he ran the game."

With Coventry having won another battle for survival, Richardson was on his way once more. "Gordon was manager by now, and he brought a few players in. Gary McAllister signed for City, and as I wasn't a regular by now, I had the chance to move. Southampton came in for me, they offered good money considering I was 35, and I was off." Richardson left Highfield Road in September 1997, after making 90 appearances for Coventry.

After gracing some of the finest stadia in the country, Richardson found Southampton's old ground at the Dell a culture shock. "It was the sort of place that when you used to go down there you'd think 'I couldn't play here every week.' There were bits of stands stuck all over the place. Odd bits of terrace, funny shapes. But David Jones, who was the manager at the time, sold it to me and I ended up loving the place."

If Southampton's ground was acceptable to the now-veteran midfielder, the club's attitude certainly wasn't. "The trouble was that they didn't have a competitive spirit. David brought in Carlton Palmer and David Hirst; Southampton were having their best run for years and we were on course for Europe. Then the club's ingrained mentality took over. It was a case of 'Okay, we've got 42 points, we're safe, let's relax.' David started changing the team round, the results slipped away and we missed out on Europe. But the people running the club still considered it a successful season because they'd stayed up."

Richardson left Southampton during that summer of 1998, moving to Barnsley, whose flirtation with the Premier League had ended unsuccessfully, and he played thirty games for them in the first division. "Me and them both were on a comedown. They were a nice club, well-run, and the manager John Hendrie brought in players like Craig Hignett and Ashley Ward, who did a job. I was there for a season and a half – we had a decent record, played in some good games. I enjoyed myself up there, even if Barnsley was a bit different from living on the south coast."

Kevin moved to Blackpool, first on loan in January 2000, then permanently two months later. There, he teamed up with former Everton midfield colleague Steve McMahon, who had just been appointed the Tangerines' manager. "I went there to help Macca out. They were bottom of the second division, and everything was a struggle. Steve managed in the same way he played, but you can't do that these days. You can't be as forceful with players, especially young ones. You have to be a bit of a father figure in some cases, but if you treated your family the way some players were treated, you'd soon be divorced."

Richardson played twenty games for Blackpool, scoring his first goal since his Villa days, before leaving in the summer of 2000 after they had failed to avoid relegation to the third division. He says of what was to prove the end of his playing career, "I trained with Darlington pre-season and waited for a club to make me an offer, but there were no takers. I was 38 and maybe they thought I was past it. But I still felt that I was fit enough and in any case, Gary McAllister was the same age and he won three trophies with Liverpool the following season."

With no club willing to employ the vastly experienced midfielder, Richardson's career as a footballer was over after over 600 games, spread over nineteen years, during which time he played for nine clubs. It was time to face up to the reality that eventually hits every former player.

"I was out of the game for three or four months, then the position of youth team coach at Sunderland came up. I was interviewed by Ian Branfoot, got offered the job and spent twelve months there. I was back working with Peter Reid and Adrian Heath again, who I'd played with at Everton, and I enjoyed my time in Sunderland.

"Then in November 2001 Carlton Palmer got the job of managing Stockport County and he offered me the chance to be his assistant. I hesitated a bit, but thought it would be part of the learning process so I took it. It was all good experience, having to learn how to deal with players' agents and putting the hours in. I was still living in Middlesbrough, so I'd find myself setting off at 5.30 am five or six days a week. I'd been there for almost two years. The chairman, Brendan Elwood, was good, the money was good, we got some decent players to sign for us and, although Carlton couldn't keep the team in the first division, everything seemed fine. Then Brendan sold the club to Brian Kennedy, who owned the Sale Sharks rugby league team, in July 2003. Carlton and Brian didn't get on, and even though we started the 2003-04 season well, we'd played seven games when things came to a head and Carlton was sacked. The chairman brought Sammy McIlroy in, and it seemed as though all our good work went down the pan."

By the time Stockport, then under the managership of Chris Turner, were relegated to League Two at the end of the 2004-05 season, Richardson had long since departed. He had been joint caretaker-manager with first team coach John Hollins after the departure of Palmer, but left when McIlroy had been given the job and brought with him his own backroom staff, amongst them another former Villa midfielder, Mark Lillis. Kevin's fortunes had, by this time, undergone a deserved upturn. "I spent almost a year out of work, waiting to be paid off by Stockport. There was a problem with that, but once it was all sorted I spoke to Mick McCarthy, and he offered me the job of reserve team manager back at Sunderland, which had just become vacant, in October 2004."

Richardson enjoyed great initial success, as his charges won the 2003-04 FA Premier League League (North) Reserve title, pipping Villa to the runner-up spot, to match their first team's clinching of the Championship. Still living near Middlesbrough, he is married with a daughter and a son, who is currently with Sunderland as an Academy pupil.

Mike Tindall

There was once a time, long before the Premier League was even thought of, when footballers knew that once their playing career was over, they would have to find alternative employment. Managerial or coaching jobs were comparatively rare; after all, a club would often in those days have forty or so players and no more than half a dozen members on the coaching staff, so the odds were stacked against a former player being able to stay in the game once his boots had been hung up for the last time.

Many fell back on the tried and trusted career of owning a pub or newsagent's shop. Others ended up as salesmen, or reps as they were more commonly known then, usually for a company which reckoned their fame would be good for business even if they knew little about the product they were selling. Many more ended their days working in factories, after finding out that their earlier achievements counted for nothing in the outside world. But, as with every walk of life, there were always a few for whom life after football turned out to be both unexpected, and fulfiling.

Born in the Birmingham suburb of Acocks Green, in 1941, Mike Tindall joined Villa straight from school, becoming a member of the ground staff in 1956. In common with many of the side that became known as the Mercer Minors, he was, in fact, signed by Joe Mercer's predecessor, Eric Houghton. It was, though, under Mercer that Tindall made his full debut, during the 1959-60 second division promotion season, after having made eight appearances for the England youth side alongside such luminaries as Bobby Moore.

In total, Mike played 135 times for Villa, scoring 10 goals. He was a competitive wing-half, who struck up a good understanding in the half-back line with Alan Deakin. "Alan was more of a defender," Tindall says, "whereas I liked to attack." Indeed, such was his appetite for getting forward that Mike scored six goals in a friendly whilst on a tour of Norway at the end of the 1959-60 season, playing at inside-left as opposed to the wing-half position into which he would later slot.

As an aside, while Villa were on that Norwegian tour after winning the second division title, they were losing out in the chase for the young Scottish wing-half Billy Bremner, who originally agreed to join the club from school but changed his mind at the last moment and signed for Leeds United instead. It's worth reflecting on how things might have worked out differently had the young Scotsman stuck to his original decision and become a Mercer Minor.

'Good old Joe' had left the Villa at the end of the 1963-64 season, after first being taken ill and then dismissed by the board once he had regained a modicum of fitness. His assistant, Dick Taylor, became manager and began the following season with Tindall in the first team. However, he suffered a broken leg in a game against Spurs in November 1964 and, although later winning back his place in the Villa side, Mike was never the same player that he had been prior to his injury. "We had a good team in the early stages, when Joe was first in charge," he reflects with pride. "There was a good blend of youth and senior players such as Peter McParland and Gerry Hitchens. I don't know how much those two would be worth now; they could both score goals."

Eventually, Tindall left Villa for Walsall during the 1967-68 season, when Villa were in the second division and Tommy Cummings in charge at Villa Park. "I had about eight managers," he says. "Tommy was a nice guy, but he shouldn't have taken the job on. He was out of his depth."

The move to Walsall was not a successful one, and Tindall made just seven appearances in the third division for the Saddlers during 1968-69, prior to leaving the professional game altogether. He looks back at his career post-Villa with some regret. "With all due respects, when you've played for the Villa you're spoilt. Walsall just aren't in that league, so playing for them could never have been the same. I'd got a couple of businesses that were doing well by then, so I decided to pack in playing full-time."

Tindall then moved to Tamworth, a regular stopping-off point for former Villa players winding down their careers during that period when pros would attempt to postpone for as long as possible the dreaded day when they gave up the game altogether. "It was a bit of a nightmare. When you go to the ground and there's just a nail to hang your coat on, you do wonder why you're there. I'd started the businesses when I was at Villa, two ladies' hairdressers. My sister ran one and my wife the other, and they were both doing well, so I didn't need the money from playing.

"I was at Tamworth for two years. In fact, John Neal asked me to play for Chester when he was manager. They were in the fourth division, but I chose Tamworth because I was thinking about the long-term and it would have meant moving away from the businesses. Maybe, looking back, I should have gone with John and stayed full-time in the Football League, but you make your decisions and have to stick by them, and that was the one I made at the time.

"After a while we sold up and moved to Sutton Coldfield. I worked for one of the Villa vice-presidents, Ron Heath, who ran Ketch Plastics in Lichfield. I was his driver for about five years, until around 1977. Then I moved back into business. I bought a fruit and veg shop at Boldmere, in partnership with a friend of ours, then later on I sold my share and we moved to Bournemouth, where I bought another, similar shop.

"We'd been there for three years and I was very settled. I thought that I was there for life, that this was what we'd be doing until we retired. Then one day my wife came home and said that she'd become a born-again Christian. I wasn't that impressed, I remember saying to her 'If that's your hobby, then good, you stick to it.' How wrong can you be?"

As he moves on to the subject of religion, Tindall becomes notably more animated. You sense that this is a story he has told many times, and that he has lost none of his enthusiasm for its telling. "I saw the difference in her, how she became a better person, a better wife and mother. She started telling me about Jesus, but I never thought much about it all. I had money, I had a home, a car; we took holidays abroad every year. I had, or so I thought, everything I needed. Why did I need Jesus?"

"Then one day I decided that I fancied running a pub. I spoke to (former Villa player) Jimmy Dugdale, and he got me up to Birmingham, where I met with someone from M&B, the brewers. I sailed through the interviews, and I got a place in Bromsgrove, the

Coach & Horses in the town centre. This was around 1983. My wife said she couldn't work there because of her beliefs, and I regret my reply to her was something that can't be found in the scriptures."

By now, Tindall had proved that not only could he accept the life of an ex-sportsman, but also that he was able to cope with the changes in business attitudes that accompanied the recession of the early eighties. However, the so-far ordered life of Mike Tindall, publican, businessman and former professional footballer, was to take one more twist, and it went in a direction that he could never have anticipated.

"The place went like a bomb for about four years. Plenty of Villa supporters used to go in there, so it was packed out most nights. We were taking a lot of money; again things seemed to be going well for me. Then, in what turned out to be my final year at the pub, another recession came along and everything went pear-shaped. It was as though someone had barricaded the doors up. Things were going badly, and my wife said to me. 'We've tried it your way, how about giving my way a try?' So I found myself on my knees in the bedroom, giving my life to Jesus. This was in February 1987; I attended church the following Sunday, for the first time ever. Ironically, the minister, Keith Blades, preached about football in Brazil, and, during the service, I could feel Jesus speaking to me. My life changed forever. I went back into the pub, the place was full and the music was blaring out. I turned the music off and announced to the customers 'Listen to me, you're all going to hell unless you are born again'."

Naturally, Tindall endured the scorn of those who failed to understand how a former footballer turned successful businessman could turn his back on the trappings of fame and fortune for a spiritual life. "All the people in the pub thought I'd gone mad. Even my own family disowned me for eighteen months. But I knew that I'd found the true meaning of life. I knew that Jesus had told me to go out and tell everyone about Him. I spent three years as a church goer, but I still felt that the Lord wished me to serve Him. Pastor Blades backed me, and I became a minister. That was fifteen years ago, and I have been doing just that ever since."

As we spoke, Mike was making final plans for a month in Kenya, preaching the gospel, as he has done for many years. "I still spend three days a week preaching in the High Street at Bromsgrove, and I've also travelled the world. It's been tough: I've been threatened, spat at, abused, and assaulted. I've also seen some horrific places. The Holocaust Museum in Jerusalem, for example. There's a truly terrifying example of the evil that man is capable of performing. But I think that my background as a footballer has helped me to withstand the abuse I receive. I could cope with 50,000 people booing me, so I can handle a few more."

The commercial-driven ethos of football must appear incompatible with Christianity, yet there are those who manage to combine both. Cyrille Regis, for example, was a founder member of Christians in Sport, while former Villa midfielder George Boateng belies his tough-tackling image on the field with a profound sense of faith. Tindall reflects on how difficult it must be to be a successful footballer whilst still preaching an ethos based on truth and forgiveness. "There is a great difficulty in combining the two. There's so much cheating in football – diving, gamesmanship, arguing with the officials. And now, of course, there's always the commercial element. When I played, the managers had the final say, but now the players are in control. Contracts are signed and easily broken when they should be upheld."

Married with three sons ("Two of them are Christians, I still haven't given up on the third"), Mike Tindall can still contrast his former time as one of the most promising wing-halves in the country four decades earlier with his role as a preacher, and has no doubt as to which of his lives he prefers. "I met some super people when I was playing. We saw some lovely places and had a great time. I was earning good money and I enjoyed spending it. But none of that compares to knowing Jesus."

Successful modern footballers don't have to worry about what they'll do when they retire. Signing just one contract with a Premier League club will make the recipient financially secure for the rest of his life. Whether they'll be as content as Mike Tindall, though, is another matter entirely.

OUT WIDE

Harry Burrows

Some former players are remembered more fondly than others, simply because they happened to be around at a time when the club were doing well. Then there are those whose contribution to the claret and blue cause is often overlooked because their best years coincided with a period when Villa were in the doldrums.

Harry Burrows belongs in the latter category. A winger talented enough to have graced the sides of a more successful era, he tends to get ignored whenever 'Best Villa XI's' are selected. Yet, had Harry been around even a few years later, when the club's remarkable journey back from the abyss was attracting worldwide comment, he would undoubtedly have qualified as an Aston Villa great.

Born in Haydock, Lancashire, in 1941, Harry Burrows left school at the age of 15 to work for the National Coal Board as a mining apprentice. He joined Villa the following year, shortly after the 1957 FA Cup final, at around the same time as many of his contemporaries who later helped form the backbone of Joe Mercer's side. Burrows played a couple of friendlies under Eric Houghton, but by the time he made his debut on the left wing for the first team, against Hull City, Houghton had been replaced by the man whose managerial career provided the greatest of all Villa Park 'if only's'. Mercer later moved to Manchester City and led them to success in all three of the major domestic trophies and the European Cup-Winners Cup.

As one of the feted Mercer Minors, Burrows made a single appearance for the England under-23 side, against Greece, in a game played at St Andrews. He was in the Villa side which played in two League Cup finals – winning the tournament in its inaugural season, 1960-61, then finishing runners-up to Birmingham City two years later – and was earmarked as the long-term Villa Park replacement for the legendary Peter McParland.

Burrows made his mark in a Villa side that, as has often been the case over the years, never fulfiled its undoubted potential. Indeed, when millionaire entrepreneur Howard Hodgson was linked with a plan to take over the club during the summer of 2003, he spoke fondly of Harry as being his boyhood idol. Hodgson initially made his fortune by building up the family business into one of the biggest undertakers in the country. "Maybe he'll give me a discount when my time comes," was Harry's reply at being informed of his place in the juvenile affections of the future tycoon.

Possessor of what has been described as a harder shot than either Stan Lynn or Dickie Dorsett, regarded as the two fiercest strikers of a ball Villa had seen for many years, Burrows looked set for a long and illustrious career in a successful Villa side. However, as the promise of Mercer's youngsters began to fade, and with the manager himself leaving the club under a cloud in the summer of 1964, so Burrows began to realise that his future lay elsewhere. He says of the time, "It was at the end of the 1963-64 season. I'd just got married and I knew for a fact that some of the players we'd been signing were on more money than I was being paid. I asked Dick Taylor, who'd just been appointed manager, if I could have an extra fiver a week. He turned me down, so I would only sign monthly contracts, as you could then. I asked for a transfer, and eventually Villa offered me the extra money, but by that time I refused. I thought 'Blow them, if they didn't want to give me the money in the first place, I don't want it now.' And I insisted on moving."

In March 1965, Burrows got his wish, signing for Stoke City, then a mid-table first division club, for the sum of £35,000. "Because I'd asked for a transfer I didn't get the 5% signing-on fee I would have been entitled to. Stoke gave me a £20 rise to join them, though, so I was very happy."

In the insane world of the Premiership, such sums are now almost incomprehensible. Indeed, as Harry comments, only half-jokingly, "It seems daft now, moving over £5 a week. Players these days probably wouldn't bother picking that much up if they dropped it on the floor."

Burrows had scored 73 goals in 181 first-team appearances for Villa, a phenomenal strike-rate for a winger, particularly at a time when the club were in such poor shape. The five pounds per week that had cost them the services of Harry Burrows was to prove a foolish saving indeed, and the board must surely have regretted their decision in the years that followed.

Burrows joined a Stoke side that, under the auspices of manager Tony Waddington, was about to embark on one of its finest periods. He remembers Waddington with fondness, "Tony was a decent bloke. In fact, he was one of the main reasons I signed for Stoke. They'd been promoted in 1963 and had managed to stay in the first division without much difficulty, but he was signing some decent players and I could tell that the club was going places. We had the likes of Dennis Viollet, Jimmy McIllroy and Maurice Setters in the side. Good, experienced players you could depend on."

Indeed, the contrast between Stoke, for so long an unheralded side yo-yoing between the divisions, and Villa, one of the aristocrats of the game, could not have been greater. "I loved the Villa, I'd have been happy to stay there if the money situation had been handled right, but there was definitely a fatalism about the place. It was as though everyone at the club knew they were on the slide and there was nothing they could do about it. Stoke, though, were totally different. They were a homely club, but they were on the up. We were top of the league at Christmas 1966, and although we slipped a bit towards the end of the season we still had the feeling that on our day we could beat anyone."

This was never proved more than in December 1966, when a Burrows-inspired Stoke side beat Villa 6-1 at the Victoria Ground, with Harry scoring a hat-trick against his old club, who would be relegated at the end of that season. "I had mixed feelings after the game," he now confesses. "I always played well against Villa, but it was a strange experience, because I had so many friends who were still there."

The wisdom of Burrows' decision to move to Staffordshire was further emphasised the following summer when the Potteries club paid fellow-Midlanders Leicester City £52,000, then a record fee for a goalkeeper, for the World Cup-winning Gordon Banks. "We were surprised when Gordon arrived, of course we were. It was a massive coup – the best goalkeeper in the world playing for Stoke. It was typical of Tony Waddington, though. Players would sign for him because he was such a good manager. And having Gordon in the side was an enormous boost. Despite all he'd done in the game there was no edge to him, he still worked as hard as ever in training. I used to send over crosses so that he could practice his handling and the concentration on his face at the end of an afternoon's training was the same as it had been in the World Cup final. Gordon made it all look so easy – there was nothing flash about him, he did everything as simply as possible."

Burrows still talks with pride about his contemporaries at the Victoria Ground. "There was George Eastham, who had helped bring about freedom of contract when he moved from Newcastle to Arsenal. He was a lovely, old-fashioned inside-forward. Then all the defence were local lads or had come through the youth team – Dennis Smith, Mike Pejic, who of course was at Villa for a while before he had to retire through injury: players like that."

While Harry Burrow was at Stoke, the club maintained a comfortable mid-table position in the top flight, never looking in danger of relegation, without ever challenging for honours in the league. Burrows played in the 1971 FA Cup semi-final, when Stoke lost 2-0 in a replay at Villa Park to eventual double-winners Arsenal. However, his career was soon to suffer a serious setback, and one from which it never fully recovered. "I was injured a couple of weeks after the semi, and I did my knee. Complications set in and in the end I was out for twelve months, which meant I missed the League Cup final the following year. I played a few games more, but I was never a regular in the first team again."

Burrows suffered the heartbreak of missing out on his club's finest hour, as Stoke beat Chelsea at Wembley, and also their brief run in the 1972-73 UEFA Cup, when they lost on aggregate in the first round to Kaiserslauten. At the end of that season, Harry moved on a free transfer to Plymouth Argyle, after a Stoke career than had taken in 245 games and seen him score 68 goals. He explains the attraction of moving to an area that has often been regarded as a footballing backwater.

"Plymouth were in the fourth division when I signed, but we managed to get promoted in my second season. Tony Waiters was the manager and, like Tony Waddington, he brought in some good players. Jim Furnell was in goal; we'd got him from Arsenal, and there was Ernie Machin, who'd been with Coventry." Also in the

Ray Graydon – who famously scored the goal which won the League Cup for Villa in 1975 – added to his silverware when guiding Walsall to the First Division via the Play-Offs.

A falling-out with Joe Mercer led to Peter McParland (bottom row, first left) making the short trip to Wolves, but injury cut his Molineux career to just 21 games.

Jim Cumbes (middle row, third from the left) had no qualms about leaving Don Howe and dropping two divisions to play for what he saw as the bigger and better supported Villa.

Ian Ormondroyd describes Graham Taylor as "by a mile the best manager I worked for". His memories of life at Boundary Park aren't quite so fond.

Paul Birch took the no-nonsense midfield play which so frustrated Lother Mattheus to the Steve Bull-dominated Wolves, linking up with two former Villa bosses in the process.

Players with contrasting views of Ron Atkinson: Kevin Richardson (top, centre) was made skipper by Big Ron, but Steve Froggatt fell out of favour with the boss over contract talks.

Both League Cup winners with Villa, Graham Fenton (left) and Shaun Teale now find their football fix in the non-league scene.

For seven yearsSammy Morgan (left) nurtured the young talent at Norwich City before taking his teaching skills to the Academy at arch rivals Ipswich.

John Gidman found Seventies superstardom at Villa and Eighties enjoyment with Big Ron, but is happy now living without football... and politicians.

A claret and blue hero twice over, if not with opposing defenders, Scottish striker Andy Lochhead still keeps tabs on the Villa from his post at Burnley.

Argyle line-up at the time was the emergent talent of Paul Mariner, who was later to go on to great fame with Ipswich, Arsenal and England, and who found Harry still able to supply a stream of crosses from which the young centre-forward could learn his trade.

The delights of the south-west were also ideal for a young family. "It was a lovely time. We lived in a beautiful area, in fact I had to keep reminding myself that I wasn't on holiday. But the travelling to away games could be a nightmare."

Argyle's promotion to the second division in 1975 was the signal for Harry to announce his retirement from football, after making nineteen appearances for the Devonian side and scoring three goals. "It was a good time to pack it in. We'd had a successful season but I was starting to struggle with injuries. I'd never had any problems before my knee, but that never fully recovered, I'd broken a few ribs and I was having problems with a hamstring. I could have gone on a bit longer, but I felt enough was enough by then. It was time to call it a day."

Like sadly too few players of the era, Harry had been making plans for retirement long before he gave serious thoughts about ceasing to play football. "I'd started a business with a partner while I was with Stoke, so I moved back to the Potteries. We were haberdashers and fabric wholesalers. The company did well, but after a time I fancied a change so I sold my share of the business and bought a pub at Congleton, Cheshire, in 1983. We were there for eleven years, and we made a good living at it until my wife and I decided that we fancied a change of direction again and started looking around for another business. We settled on a sub-post office in Abbots Bromley, Staffordshire, and we've been there ever since."

Their three children now grown up, Harry and his wife continue to run the post office in the quiet village they have made their home for the past ten years. Doling out the stamps and pensions, Harry looks the typical shopkeeper. Unless they were keen football followers themselves, few of his customers would guess that their friendly sub-postmaster had a playing career that lasted almost twenty years, most of it spent in the top flight, represented his country and played on the winning side in a cup final. Indeed, I'd visited the shop myself several times when visiting family in the area and never had the slightest inkling that the man who'd served me had once been a hero of the Villa Park crowd, until a chance remark linked 'Harry from the post office' with Harry Burrows the Villa star of the sixties. Which is hardly surprising; players from what now seems a bygone age, before footballers became front-page celebrities, rarely boast of their experiences, even if, like Harry Burrows, they have ample reason to do so.

Stephen Froggatt

Steve Froggatt enjoyed a strange Villa career. He was never tipped for great things as a youth player, yet became a first team regular while still in his teens. He did well in one of Villa's most fondly-regarded sides of the modern era, although there was no great furore when he was sold with his best years obviously still to come. He made less than fifty first-team appearances, but remains as well-remembered as players who were with the club for much longer.

Steve was born in Lincoln in 1973, and first came to Villa Park at the age of thirteen. "I'd spend holidays training with the schoolboy players, then I signed YTS forms when I left school in 1989. The Villa put me into digs with a big Irish family, the Tyrells, and it was the best thing that could have happened to me. I was a very shy young lad, but being with this family helped me develop as a more outgoing character. I'd have found it a lot harder to make the grade otherwise. Mrs Tyrell was a lovely lady who died at the beginning of 2005. I owed her a great deal."

Joining Villa during the reign of Graham Taylor, like many other youngsters of the time he found that the first-team manager took more of an interest in his younger charges than would have been the case at most clubs. "Graham made me feel at home. There was a connection between us because we were both from the same area. Graham was from Scunthorpe and had spent a lot of his playing career with Lincoln and then managed them."

Froggatt was part of a highly-successful crop of Villa youngsters that came through a policy revived by Taylor and his youth development officer, Dave Richardson. He speaks with obvious warmth of the success that the club enjoyed in bringing quality youngsters through the ranks. "They did a great job. I played with Dwight Yorke, Bryan Small, Graham Fenton; then there were people such as

Martin Carruthers and Tommy Mooney who had long careers with other clubs."

With Taylor leaving to manage England and Jo Venglos a short-term appointment, the arrival of Ron Atkinson was to be a significant time for a player who, almost unheralded, was becoming one of the most promising young wingers in the country. "Ron was fantastic. We were playing West Ham on Boxing Day, 1991, and he told me the day before that I was going to be on the bench. We were staying in a hotel and I couldn't sleep, with the excitement and the noise from the Christmas parties that were going on. I was buzzing all the way through matchday, then Ron put me on with ten minutes to go. I ran around like a mad thing and I don't think I touched the ball, but it was the best Christmas present I ever had."

Froggatt did well enough to make several appearances as the season wore on, and soon found himself the centre of more attention than he thought possible. "Within a month I scored against Swindon in the FA Cup, live on Match of the Day; then I got called into the England under-21 side, won the Barclays Young Player of the Month and got the Man of the Match award when we played Everton at Villa Park. It was unbelievable. Suddenly people were stopping me in the street and wanting to talk."

Such progress did, however, have its downside. "Ron had the ability to make you feel ten feet tall. However, I was always rushed back into the squad after I'd had an injury. At that time I thought it was an honour to be so vital to the team, but looking back I question the wisdom of it. I'd already started to have problems with my left ankle, and I'm convinced that playing when I wasn't 100% weakened it."

The following season saw Villa playing a brand of football that won them plaudits at every turn, even if they were to finish trophyless. For Steve Froggatt, making the bullets for the sensational striking duo of Dean Saunders and Dalian Atkinson to fire in spectacular fashion, success came at a price. "First I got a knock from Gavin Peacock, of Queens Park Rangers, then we played Wimbledon in the game where Dalian Atkinson scored THAT goal. I skipped past Warren Barton in the first minute and crossed the ball for Dean Saunders to put us one up. Vinny Jones came over and said that if I did it again I'd end up in row Z. So me and Tony Daley did a few more runs down the wing and I ended up being stretchered off. I never did learn to duck out of a tackle; that was my weakness."

The highlight of the following season came with the Coca-Cola Cup final victory over Manchester United. However, for Steve it marked the beginning of what would prove to be a premature departure from Villa Park. "It all began with a dispute about money. I'd been earning £25 a week as a YTS trainee. Then, on my first pro contract, I was paid £175 and finally £300 a week. I was an established England under-21 international and there were kids coming through who were being paid more than I was.

"Ron had got me signed up with Jerome Anderson as my agent, but I felt they weren't right for me. I was offered an embarrassing contract and that was when I knew that I would be leaving. I'd heard rumours that something wasn't right, so my dad helped me looked for another agent. Ron tried to pressurise me into signing the contract, but it was only for two years and the money was terrible. I wanted to stay, and I thought the club would come back with a better offer. I felt as though I belonged at Villa. I'd been with them when I was still at school; I wanted to stay there forever."

Most of the talk at Villa Park was concerned with the upcoming cup final, but Froggatt had additional concerns. "I still hadn't signed, and then I got injured. I missed the semis against Tranmere, but played in the last few games before the final – so I fancied my chances of being in the team for Wembley, or at least on the bench. Then out of the blue, Ron said to me, 'If you don't sign your new contract you won't be in the team for the final.'

"I thought he was bluffing, but he wasn't. He told us the line-up a couple of days before the match and Graham Fenton was in the side. I was delighted for Graham, but when the substitutes were named and both Dwight and I were out, I was desolate. Both of us could have come off the bench if things were going wrong, but the players Ron did pick were never going to be able to have an influence. Nigel Spink and Kevin Richardson, the senior pros, were great with me, telling me not to worry and to get over the disappointment, but that was the first realisation I had that football's a tough game, and when it comes to the crunch, you're on your own."

Ron Atkinson may have disappointed Froggatt, but he wasn't going to get away completely scot-free. "Ron had put a crate of

Courvoisier brandy in the dressing room, and Dwight sneaked a bottle out with us as we left before the game. We sat there on the bench all through the match drinking five star brandy out of plastic cups. It was the best day I've had that I haven't played a part in, but later on, when the team were celebrating, Dwight and I sneaked off to drown our sorrows in private."

For Froggatt, the treatment he was experiencing at the hands of Atkinson hadn't yet finished. "We played Everton at Villa Park three days later, and I was back in the side. I was also the only player in the squad not to get a medal from the final. That was it with Ron for me. Not only had he stitched me up over the final, he'd also behaved so pettily. I'm ashamed to say, it but I hardly tried for the rest of the season. We went on tour to South Africa and I never tried. I wasn't interested in playing for Villa, my contract was undecided and Ron went off to work for ITV at the World Cup. I didn't have a clue what had gone wrong – I'd gone from his golden boy to being a pariah."

There may still have been a way for Froggatt to stay at Villa Park, and potential salvation was from an oft-maligned source. "Doug Ellis was great to me. He couldn't believe the story when I told him what had happened and he eventually offered me big money to stay, but I wanted out. Whatever people might say about him, and whatever he might get up to, Doug was great with me. Just about the only regret I had over leaving Villa was that I disappointed him by going. I have to say, though, that whatever problems I had with Ron are all in the past. We get on perfectly well now and I have nothing but respect for him."

Unlikely though it may have seemed for a highly-rated 21 year-old, Froggatt had no qualms about dropping a division to sign for Wolves in a £1.1 million deal. "Graham Taylor was manager, my best mate Tony Daley had just signed for them as well, Sir Jack Hayward was bankrolling another promotion bid and I wanted to be a part of history as one of the players who got Wolves back into the big time." He had played in just 36 games for Villa, scoring three goals.

Froggatt and Daley might have been the big signings, but throughout the nineties there was only one man who was the star at Molineux. "I thought I might have had a problem with Steve Bull, but although he was wary at first, we became big mates. You have to earn Bully's respect and work for the team. It all helped towards a great team spirit."

Froggatt and Wolves began 1994-95 in confident mood, but things soon turned sour for all concerned as the club yet again failed to capitalise on a good start. "We were going well and we were top of the league at Christmas. Then we lost Tony with a bad injury, John de Wolf was out, as was Neil Emblen, and I got injured. The board should have replaced us all, but they didn't. Getting into the play-offs was a great achievement with the amount of injuries in the squad, but Bolton were too much for us in the semi-finals. Graham couldn't be blamed for that, then things went wrong for him over the summer."

Indeed they did, as a planned move by Bull to Coventry City broke down, and, in the aftermath of the failed transfer, Taylor was seen as the man who was driving the icon of Wolverhampton away from the club, as a punishment, some said, for a perceived slight by the striker when Taylor was England manager. It was later revealed that the board had sanctioned the sale of Bull to Coventry, and had shifted the blame on to Taylor in an attempt to avoid criticism of themselves.

But with hindsight, the deal would have been a shrewd one for all concerned, as Froggatt explains. "Steve's best years were coming to an end. Coventry had offered £2 million, which was good money, and he could have played in the Premiership at last. It was a good deal all round, but it fell through and the fans never forgave Graham. Logically it was a good piece of business, but football supporters don't always think logically."

Wolves started off the following season badly and, with supporter unrest growing, Taylor's resignation soon became inevitable. It is now generally accepted that Bull's influence was allowed to grow too strong at Molineux and that Taylor was driven out too soon. Froggatt concurs with both assertions.

"Steve (Bull) had been a phenomenon. If it wasn't for him, Wolves might have gone out of business. Yet he had to have the team built round him, and because he was impossible to drop, good players such as David Kelly and Don Goodman were sold because they couldn't work with him. Graham saw that Steve wasn't indispensable, and for that he lost his job."

However, by the time Taylor left for what was to be the renaissance of his career at Watford, football had become one of the least of Steve Froggatt's worries. "I nearly died," he says with remarkable matter of factness. "I got injured playing against Reading. Martin Taylor hit me; there was no malice in his challenge, although it looked horrific on TV. I recovered from the initial injury, and got back into the team, but then I started losing weight. I looked terrible, and eventually I said that I wasn't fit for the next match and collapsed. I was taken to hospital and the doctors found out that I had a double femoral vein in my thigh, which only happens in something like one in ten million people, and that I had a blood clot in one of the veins. Normally it would have been picked up right away, but because I had a double vein the blood was flowing normally through the other vein and the problem wasn't noticeable. If the clot had travelled I would have been in real trouble. In fact, I was told that if I'd have played another game I could have died.

"I'd been out for three or four months with the original injury, then another five months with the clot problem. I was in hospital when Graham resigned and I felt bad about that. I have so much respect for him; I was so sorry that I couldn't help him when he needed it."

Like most of the players Taylor has dealt with, Froggatt has evidence of how his former manager cared for much more than his first team and their footballing performance. "I could never keep my shinpads on, because my calves were so thin. Then I went in to training one day and there he was, with a blackboard. Written on there were seven ways to tie up shinpads and he told me that I'd be fined a week's wages if I ever let them come loose again. I didn't.

"While Graham was with Wolves I was getting married. He asked me if I was sure about what I was doing, if I was happy, and if I could afford the house we were buying. I said that everything was fine and he asked, 'So who was that blonde woman who was in your house yesterday?' He'd gone round to check my home and everything else out. I thought it was a bit strange, but it was part of his philosophy that a happy player will always be more likely to perform well than one who has problems. He was the most honest, hard-working man you could ever meet. And the blonde woman was someone from the estate agents."

Froggatt made a full recovery from his injury problems, playing in most of the club's games as they reached the play-offs in 1997, only to lose to Crystal Palace, a defeat that inspired club owner Sir Jack Hayward to make his 'Golden Tit' speech, in which he stated that no longer would he bankroll under-performing players who saw Wolves as an easy pay-day where high wages and failure were natural bedfellows.

Of that period in his career, Steve says, "I loved my time at Wolves. I had some good friends there, we got to the play-offs and reached the FA Cup semi-final in 1998. With a bit more luck we could have been really successful. But I was headed for the last year of my contract and they decided to sell me, because Sir Jack had decided that he wasn't going to finance the club indefinitely, and Robbie Keane and myself were the two most saleable players. I was in my best form ever, so I thought I deserved at least a three-year deal, but they would only give me one year, so I had to go." Froggatt had played 106 league games for Wolves, scoring 9 goals, and a transfer fee of £1.9 million was set by the board.

"It would have been nice to go back to Villa, but John Gregory didn't come in for me, and in the end I had the choice of Derby, Middlesbrough or Coventry. I chose Coventry, because Gordon Strachan, who I had a lot of time for, was manager and also because I didn't have to move house. We had a two year old and my wife was pregnant again, so that was a big consideration in my choice. Looking at how Coventry did and how well Middlesbrough are performing it might look as though I made the wrong decision, but I was happy at Coventry."

Moving to Highfield Road might have been a problem for an ex-Villa player, especially at such a time, when it seemed as though Villa were cherry-picking Coventry's star names, but Froggatt was unaware of any such difficulty. "On the day I signed, in September 1998, one of the press boys said 'You've come from the other side and we're playing them on Saturday. What's your feelings on that?' It was the first time I'd ever known anything about it. As far as I was concerned Coventry were just another club and Villa didn't bother with them. Even Walsall would be a bigger game for Villa."

However, Froggatt's return to the top flight was not to be easy. "We lost 2-1 at home to Villa, which didn't help, and to be honest I made a poor start. I'd been out of the Premier League for four years and the game had changed tremendously. There'd been a big influx of foreign players and I was like a little boy lost for the first few weeks. I got a bit of stick from the fans but gradually my performances improved and I ended up being called into the England squad for the Euro 2000 play-offs against Scotland."

Coventry were one of many clubs to be spending money they hadn't got and couldn't afford, in an attempt to make progress up the Premiership table. Ever the astute player, Froggatt could see that this policy wasn't working. "It was obvious that they were spending too much. Gordon put together three separate teams in the time I was there – he had to sell every player who they had a reasonable offer for. He never had a chance of putting a successful side together; it must have been frustrating for him. It was the same when Ron was manager. He was trying to sign big name players on gates of twenty thousand. "

Froggatt's call-up to the England squad was just one of the plus points in his life as 1999 came to an end. "I was on the bench for the play-off first leg at Hampden Park. That was an awesome experience, but my wife was due to give birth at any time, so Kevin Keegan let me come home during the week rather than stay with the squad. Luckily it was a quick labour. She gave birth to our son, and I drove back to the squad hotel to find that Kevin had bought me a jeroboam of champagne. Then I sat down that evening to dinner and talked all night with David Beckham about babies."

However, there was a downside to all this attention, and it would cause Froggatt one of the biggest regrets of his career. "When you're involved with internationals everyone wants to know you. My phone never stopped ringing, although my first concern was for my family. Kevin was great, but he could see that I was knackered, so he dropped me from the bench for the second leg at Wembley, promising that I would be given a run-out in the upcoming friendlies. England lost the game 1-0, although we went through 2-1 on aggregate, and after the game Kevin said 'I should have picked you'. I was glad he hadn't at the time, because I wouldn't have been able to do much, but with what came afterwards I wish I'd have got a game."

A few weeks later, Froggatt suffered what was to be a crushing blow to his career. "We were playing Sunderland, and with seven minutes gone, Nicky Summerbee came in and did me. We had a history – Tony Daley and I used to run him ragged every time we played, and this time he deliberately caught me. I tried to come back, but after three games, we were playing Villa and Ugo caught me again, which shattered my ankle completely. That was an accident, but Summerbee's was deliberate. That's life, though. I've got every reason to be bitter, but you get on with life. I'm a great believer in fate, and that was mine."

Froggatt spent over a year attempting to recover, but deep down, he knew that his career was over. The end came in May 2001, a few days after Coventry, who had defied relegation so many times over the years, finally dropped to the first division. He had played 54 games for the Sky Blues, scoring five goals. "I had another ligament reconstruction on my left ankle, but no-one has ever come back and played after having the same job done twice. Nobody told me this, and I was still determined to make a comeback. Stewart Collie, who was Coventry's physiotherapist, stopped me from sinking into depression, then one day I said to him, 'I'll never play again, will I?' His expression told me everything – the staff at the club had known for a long time, but they were waiting for me to accept the inevitable before they told me."

Once his retirement had been announced, Froggatt, whose father died shortly afterwards during what was obviously a traumatic time for one of football's genuinely nice guys, spent a year reflecting on what the future held. "I was lucky, I didn't have any financial worries, but I just wanted to spend some time with my family and get my head around not playing again."

Then fate lent a hand in the shape of the then-head of sport at Radio WM, Tim Beech. "Tim asked me if I would like to do some commentary work. I'd always been willing to talk to the press when I'd played, which might have been the reason why he asked me. I did a bit of work for WM, enjoyed it, and then started summarising for Five Live. Pat Murphy, their main man in the region, got on to his bosses and said they should use me because I was honest, which was nice of him, but it was true. Most of the time they have managers or other people still involved in the game commenting on matches and it's hard for them to give an objective opinion because they might end up having to deal with the club or the players they're talking about the next week." Murphy, himself one of the most respected broadcasters in sport, remains happy with the work of his protégé. "He sounds distinctive, which is essential on radio. That Lincolnshire accent goes down well with listeners. Steve's also kept in touch with the modern game and isn't afraid to speak his mind."

Experienced media professionals may have resented the arrival of Froggatt on their turf, but he never found this a problem, "I'd always helped them in the past, so they were fine with me. The money's not great, but it's a good part-time job and it also fills the time." Indeed, as one regular in the Midlands press boxes says of Froggatt, "You could tell from the start that here was that rare thing – a well educated former footballer. Steve says what he thinks and doesn't get bogged down in footballing cliché."

Froggatt admits that he has been lucky to find an outlet that keeps him in contact with the game. "The problem for many players when they give up football is keeping busy. You go from a job where you're doing what you love, where the money's fabulous and the hours are short, then suddenly, you've got nothing. I firmly believe that the PFA should do more to help players once their career is over. They do some good work with helping players get coaching qualifications, but how many coaching jobs are there? In any case, getting into coaching or management is a lottery. You need a bit of luck, and there's very often a touch of the old pals act. Not that I was worried – it wasn't something I ever fancied doing. Now I work for the BBC, I do Central Soccer Special, and I used to write a column for the *Sunday Mercury*, but I packed that in because they asked me to be more controversial, which isn't my way of doing things. I've been asked to do a training course for journalists at university, which is something I'm thinking about"

In addition to his media work, Froggatt has set up a financial services company, which, amongst other things, advises young footballers on how to handle their considerable earnings. "They're always asking my advice, and I say 'Whatever you earn, look after it, because it isn't going to last forever.' I suppose I could set up as an agent, but that's not something I fancy doing at present"

Despite only playing in a handful of games for Villa, there's no doubt which club Steve Froggatt regards as his first love. "Every time I go back to Villa Park, it's like going back home. A lot of the people are still there from when I was playing and it feels like I've never been away."

Married with two children to a former Miss Aston Villa, who he met when he was a judge in the competition ("There was nothing untoward going on; I didn't vote for her. I thought she was the fourth-best of the lot"), Steve lives near Lichfield. The player who BBC broadcaster Stuart Linnell once described as "The nicest man in football," remains as bright and effervescent as he ever did on the pitch. He might have been unlucky in his playing career, but if he feels any resentment at the way things turned out, Stephen Froggatt certainly hides it well.

Ray Graydon

Nothing better sums up Villa's ambitions when they were in the third division than the number of players signed during that time who were still more than capable of holding their own when the club returned to its rightful place in the top flight. All retain a special place in the affections of Villa supporters, and none more so than Ray Graydon.

Born in July 1947, Ray left school in his hometown of Bristol at the age of fifteen. "I worked in a brush factory, running the warehouse. I'd been offered a job in a shoe shop, but when the manager told me I had to work on Saturdays, I said that football was more important than the job. 'Not in the real world,' he replied. Well, I've been in football for more than forty years, so he was wrong there."

Graydon took his place in that real world for eighteen months, before being offered an apprenticeship with Bristol Rovers. "I'd been getting up at 6.15, catching the bus, walking another three miles to work, then two nights a week I was travelling for another two hours there and back to train with Bristol City. They didn't seem interested in taking me on, but Rovers offered a trial and signed me at the end, along with ten others. I have to say, though, that in the year I was an apprentice I didn't make much progress. Playing football for a living wasn't as enjoyable as playing for fun, and I wasn't surprised when Rovers let me go. What I didn't know at the time, though, was that my dad had spoken to Bill Dodgin, who was on the coaching staff, and when Bill said that I was being let go, my dad said, 'He'll prove you wrong'."

Graydon could so easily have become one of the legion of former apprentices who failed to make the grade and slipped out of football altogether, but he was determined to overcome this setback, although not without remembering to have a fall-back should his playing situation not improve. "I was the only one of the eleven apprentices at Rovers who went to school for a day a week, and I began training as an electrical engineer, so when I finished my footballing apprenticeship I began one as an electrician. I signed for an amateur team in Bristol, called Hanbrook FC, and did well enough with them to get into the England under-18 side.

"A few months later, Rovers asked me to play a few youth games, then I was picked for their reserves. In my last reserve game, at St Andrews, Birmingham moved the legendary veteran Stan Lynn, who'd played hundreds of games for Villa and Blues, over to leftback to mark me, and the Rovers manager, Bert Tann, was so impressed that he signed me afterwards as a part-time professional. I joined at the same time as Larry Lloyd, who played for Liverpool and England, then won the European Cup with Forest. I was on £5 10 shillings a week, and when I was 21, the manager, who by this time was Fred Ford, asked me to sign as a full-time pro on £20 a week.

Graydon soon made his name as a goalscoring winger, netting 33 times in 133 appearances for Rovers, before being called in by his manager, who by this time was Bill Dodgin, one day in 1971. "As soon as I got there, he said 'Guess who's after you?' Being ambitious, I thought it might be Arsenal or Manchester United, and when he told me it was Villa, my first reaction was that they were in the third division, as we were. I wasn't too keen on moving as I'd just got married. So I picked up my dad from working on the night shift in my old Austin A40, and for the first time ever I asked his advice about something vital. 'Get yourself up there as quickly as you can,' he replied. 'Aston Villa are massive.' And with that, and the promise from him that he and my mother would still come and watch me, I agreed to sign."

The deal that took Graydon to Villa Park was worth £40,000, but included Villa captain Brian Godfrey moving to Eastville. As is often the case in such situations, the move was not a popular one with Villa supporters, who regarded Godfrey as the hero of the previous season's run to the League Cup final at Wembley. Graydon admits that he was hardly welcomed with open arms; "When Vic Crowe signed me I had a bit of trouble winning the fans over, and they let me know about it, but I managed to get them on my side before too long. Then we won the third division, got promoted a couple of years later and I scored 27 goals in the season. Forwards wouldn't get that many now."

Graydon's brief description of those days skipped over a few salient facts, such as the fifteen goals he scored when Villa won the third division, including a memorable performance against his old club, Rovers. The injured George Curtis was asked by Crowe to watch Graydon from the main stand at Eastville and provide a detailed analysis of his game. Ray promptly laid on a goal for Andy Lochhead in the first few minutes and then he and Willie Anderson gave further credence to their reputation as the finest pair of wingers outside the first division with a dazzling display. There was also the memorable match against second division leaders Manchester United at Villa Park, as the promotion battle of 1974-75 was reaching what would prove to be a successful climax. Graydon opened the scoring after four minutes and lead Villa to such a convincing win that most of the travelling United support had left before the end.

Graydon was, indeed, top scorer in the second division when Villa blazed their way to promotion in 1975. He also scored the winning goal in that season's League Cup final, and helped, amongst others, Brian Little, who earned a place in the England team on the back of 24 goals, many of which were created by his colleague on the right wing.

As Villa established themselves in the first division over the next two years, Graydon further entered the record books, as the scorer of the club's first goal in European competition, during a 4-1 defeat away at Royal Antwerp in the UEFA Cup, and then as a member of the side that finally overcame Everton in the second replay of the 1977 League Cup final. He remembers the time with fondness. "My father died at the age of 54. By that time he'd seen me become established in the Villa side, score the winner in a Wembley final and play regularly in the first division."

By the time Graydon won his second League Cup winner's tankard he had become resigned to bit-part status in the Villa side that had provided so much entertainment throughout 1976-77. "I'd been injured early on in the season against Albion. Len Cantello had caught me, and my knee ligaments were damaged. It was a fair tackle; I don't blame Len, although with what happened in our games with Albion round about that time, there were naturally those who said he'd fouled me deliberately. I was out for twelve weeks, which was the longest I ever missed through injury throughout my career, and when I came back, Ron Saunders had settled on the three-man attack of John Deehan, Brian Little and Andy Gray, which did well for him. Then, at the end of the season, when I was coming up to thirty, he told me that I wasn't part of his plans, which was fair enough." By then, Graydon had played 223 league games for the Villa, scoring 81 goals, a ratio which puts him in such exalted company as Peter McParland and Harry Burrows. This figure is even more praiseworthy when taking into consideration the fact that throughout the seventies, wingers were increasingly becoming as rare as a strike-free week at Longbridge.

Of his eventual move from Villa Park, Ray recalls a time when his knowledge of the game was not all it might have been. "Frank McLintock wanted to sign me for Leicester City. I spoke to him, and he also asked me what I thought of Kenny Burns, who was then at Birmingham. I said, 'He's a bit of a rough house. I'd be careful if I were you.' Frank didn't sign Kenny, Brian Clough stepped in and in the next three years he won the league, two European Cups and the PFA Player of the Year award. I know a lot about football, don't I?"

Ray eventually moved to Coventry, but spent less than a season there. "Gordon Milne was manager, with Ron Wylie as his coach. Ron had been Vic Crowe's assistant at Villa, so I had at least one familiar face that I was working with." However, a recurrence of his knee problems restricted Ray to just twenty first-team appearances and five goals in 1977-78, and before the end of the season he followed the path of many of his contemporaries, across the Atlantic, to play in the NASL for Washington Diplomats. "The manager was Gordon Bradley, who had signed Pele for New York Cosmos. It was an experience to play over there, but I missed England so, despite having signed for three years, we moved back after a summer."

Back in England, Ray moved to Oxford United, then of the third division, in time for the 1978-79 season. "Fred Ford, my old boss at Bristol Rovers, was the youth-team coach, and Mick Brown the manager. I played for three seasons, but was still having some injury problems and finally retired from playing in 1981. By then, I'd moved into the coaching side. Fred was taken ill, and I took over his job as coach. I was lucky enough to be kept on by several managers, as Oxford moved through the divisions." Graydon played 42 games for Oxford, scoring ten goals. His total league career, over a period of fifteen years, stretched to 387 games, and he scored 116 goals. Few wingers before or since can boast such a record.

Meanwhile, Oxford's status improved at a rate that has never since been equalled. They made history when winning the third division title in 1983-84 and becoming second division champions the following season. By now, the club were under the ownership of controversial businessman Robert Maxwell. Graydon, though, had little to do with the larger than life Czech who oversaw the club's meteoric rise. "I'm sure there's a book that could be written just about the time he owned Oxford, but he was always alright with me. Whatever he got up to elsewhere, what he did with Oxford was a magnificent achievement. We went from the third straight to the first and won the League Cup, almost mirroring what Villa did. What made it more impressive, though, was that Villa had massive gates so they could spend big money. Oxford had hardly any support when we started and we had to find our own players."

And find them, they did. Such names as John Aldridge, Dean Saunders and Ray Houghton first made their names at the ramshackle Manor Ground. Graydon was a witness to the club's now-famous exit from the Milk Cup of 1984, when Everton saved the tie and Howard Kendall's job with an equaliser at the Manor in the quarter-final, and also to Oxford's defeat of Villa in the semi-finals of the same competition two season later.

Graham Turner's Villa side, expected to prove too good for the newly-promoted Oxford, yet were themselves brushed aside with ease. Graydon says of the tie, "I always expected us to get through. We had a good side and we could give anyone a game on our day. I took two good teams, first to the Daily Express five-a-side title at Wembley Arena and then we won a six-a-side tournament against the other clubs in the first division at the NEC. They might not have meant much, but there were some good players in the opposition and no player at that level wants to lose, whatever the occasion."

By now, Graydon had worked his way through the behind-the-scenes ranks at Oxford and was assistant manager to Maurice Evans. "I'd been with Jim Smith, who was a great bloke to work for.

Then, when we got promotion to the first division he left to take the job at QPR and asked me to join him. I turned the offer down, and stayed with Oxford, as number two to Maurice Evans. I was proved right when we beat Rangers in the League Cup final the following March."

To win at Wembley in front of over 90,000 supporters must have been a huge frustration for the management of a club whose average gates were a fraction of that amount, even allowing for the limited room at the Manor Ground. "They just couldn't get enough people in. They'd made a few improvements, which made the place appear less ramshackle, but they still couldn't get many supporters inside," explains Ray. Anyone who attended a game at the ground, particularly standing in the open-air away section where being able to see both goals was a bonus, could have been forgiven for not wishing to make a repeat visit, but the unwelcoming appearance of the Manor Ground certainly added to Oxford's problems and made their sojourn in the top flight all the more remarkable.

It's one of football's great ironies that a manager who takes a club beyond their previous capabilities can often be the first to suffer when they begin to find their own level again. Getting Oxford into the first division had been a magnificent achievement, and keeping them there equally praiseworthy. However, Maurice Evans's reward when Oxford finally looked like surrendering their top-flight status was dismissal in March 1988. This was to prove the end of Ray Graydon's nine-year association with Oxford United, as he explains: "I spoke to Robert Maxwell's son, Kevin, who was running the club, because naturally enough I wanted to take over from Maurice. I'd been there long enough, and I knew I could do the job. Then Mark Lawrenson was appointed. I spoke to him one Friday night and he was keen for me to stay on, but I decided that he would want things done differently and so I decided to leave."

Graydon's next stop was Watford, another one of football's traditional lesser lights who had achieved a meteoric rise through the divisions, and who, by coincidence, were relegated from the first division at the same time as Oxford at the end of the 1987-88 season. "Steve Harrison, who was their manager, wanted me to join him as youth-team coach. I was at Vicarage Road for a couple of years and we brought David James through as well as winning the FA

Youth Cup. Chris Nicholl then asked me to be his reserve-team coach at Southampton and I was there for eight years. I worked for Chris, and when he left I was with Ian Branfoot, Alan Ball and finally, Dave Merrington. Graeme Souness became manager in 1997 and he had a big clear-out so I left."

In his time at Southampton, Graydon yet again played his part in helping a small club to stay in the top flight against the odds. "We brought some good players through the ranks. Alan Shearer, Francis Benali, Billy Dodds, players like that. We won the Football Combination league and cup, which might not sound too prestigious, but we were competing against the likes of Arsenal and Chelsea, with their big squads. I also caught up again with Matt le Tissier. He'd been training with us at Oxford when he was a youngster, but he chose to sign for Southampton.

"There was always a feeling, not of inferiority, but of pride that Southampton managed to stay up every year. It was as though the club never quite felt it belonged until they moved to St Mary's, and, ironically, that was when they got relegated."

"I was out of the game for a while, although I had several opportunities to return. I was offered the job of reserve team coach at Portsmouth, while Graham Taylor wanted me to oversee all the club's coaching when he went back to Watford. In the end, I spent a season with Queens Park Rangers, looking after their youth set-up, then moved to Port Vale as assistant manager to John Rudge. I helped Vale avoid relegation, but the job as manager of Walsall came up in 1999 and I successfully applied for that."

Graydon's assistant at Walsall was his old Southampton boss and, more pertinently, Villa team-mate Chris Nicholl. Both men played for Vic Crowe and his assistant Ron Wylie in a team that produced more than its fair share of future managers. In addition to Graydon and Nicholl, their team-mates such as Bruce Rioch, Ian Ross and the Little brothers, Alan and Brian, went on to enjoy long and often successful managerial careers. Was this, I wondered, down to the virtues instilled in them by the often under-rated Crowe? "I'm not sure. Myself, Chris and Bruce used to spend a lot of time together after training. It was like the situation in the sixties at West Ham, when Malcolm Allison and his team-mates became bosses themselves. We'd go to Ernie's Café at the bottom of Carriage Drive at

Villa Park, and we'd talk about football. Ernie was a bit of a shady character, but he was glad of our custom and I think it was there, more than anywhere else, that we started out on the road to becoming managers."

"That's not to say that I didn't learn from the managers I played for. Vic was very good at understanding private matters. You could talk to him about any problems you might have, while Ron Wylie was purely a football man. Then came Ron Saunders, who always used the senior players to help him out with coaching sessions."

Graydon's time at Walsall saw yet more success as the West Midlands' favourite other team gained promotion to the first division, were relegated and then came straight back up via the play-offs. Ray beams with pride as he recalls the afternoon in Cardiff that has gone down as the greatest day in the club's history. "That was as good as I've ever had in football. We played Reading, and they had twice as many supporters at the Millennium Stadium as we did. They went ahead, and although we equalised we were down to ten men because we'd made our substitutions, with Don Goodman looking as though he'd given his all. Then we went a goal down in extra-time and Don, at wing-back, started to run the show. After the match I had so many letters from people telling me about family members who had followed Walsall all their lives and had never known a day like it. It was very touching."

Unfortunately for Graydon, Walsall showed as much desire to return to the second division as they had on other occasions when they had been promoted, and he lost his job in January 2002, ironically on the day before John Gregory walked out as manager of Villa. Many felt that Ray had been unfairly treated, both by the board, who sacked him, and by some of the supporters, whose criticism of the manager who had done so well for them was seen as short-sighted. "One of the problems at Walsall is that their higher position got them a lot of new supporters who hadn't been around during the bad times, so they wanted to know why we were struggling. I was told that it happens all the time when Walsall are in that position. When you consider that in my final season they were competing with teams such as Manchester City, Sheffield Wednesday and Coventry, all of them established top division sides not long before, you can see how hard it was to stay up."

But, despite his dismissal as Walsall manger, Graydon retains no hard feelings towards the club and its hierarchy. "I enjoyed my time there and Jeff Bonser, the chairman, is still a friend. Whenever I go back to Bescot, I always feel at home."

Ray then made the move back to where his professional football career had begun, almost forty years earlier. "I'd never really thought about returning to Bristol Rovers. It hadn't been a great ambition of mine to become their manager, but the opportunity arose and I gave it a go. Rovers were in trouble at the bottom of the third division when I joined, but I signed my old Walsall player, Andy Rammell, and he helped us to stay up. The following season, we were pushing for the play-off places and the opportunity was there to sign players and move on, but there was no backing from the board and the momentum was lost."

Graydon was sacked in January 2004, with Rovers twelfth in division three. Under, first, the temporary control of club coach Phil Bater and then joint – also temporary, until the end of the season – managership of Russell Osman and Kevin Broadhurst, they narrowly avoided relegation to the Conference. Graydon, naturally, remains bitter about this turn of events. "If I'd have had some help when it was needed I'd have got Bristol Rovers to the play-offs. As it was, I took them from fighting relegation to pushing for promotion, reduced their debts and knocked a million pounds off the wage bill. In any ordinary business, that would have been called shrewd management." Even after the dust has settled from his dismissal, Graydon remains angry at the turn of events, "The people at Rovers remain just about the only people in football that I don't get on with. In the end I had to call in the League Managers' Association to help get the compensation that I'd agreed with them. It was a messy business, and very sad."

At an age when many people in football are thinking of winding down their career, Ray found himself faced with a complete change in focus. "Mickey Adams asked me to work with him at Leicester, but I said that I was going away on holiday with my wife; it was the first time we'd ever had the chance to go away during the football season. Then Howard Wilkinson rang me while we were in Tenerife and asked if I fancied spending some time as his assistant in China."

The job was with Chinese champions Shanghai Shenua, and Graydon's work soon showed the contrast with his previous employment. "Within the first week I was flying out to Japan to watch Iwati, who we were playing in the Asian Champions League. Then after that it was back to Shanghai for the league programme. The game was taking off, as was the Chinese economy. We had massive grounds, the stadium was huge and you could see how the country was growing. We'd be in Shanghai, with the skyscrapers and the modern buildings, then go out into the country and still see the poverty. Where Paul Gascoigne played for a while, that was an awful place. The distances we travelled as well; we were flying almost everywhere. It was like it was when I was playing in America back in 1978."

Graydon returned to England, and began working for the League Managers Association, chaired by John Barnwell, as an area rep. "There are four of us - Terry Dolan, Frank Clarke, Bryan Flynn and myself. In the past, managers have only contacted the LMA when they were in trouble, but it's now our job to liaise with them all the time.

And the start of the 2005-06 season saw Ray Graydon as a trailblazer in another aspect of the football world's ever-expanding role as a branch of the leisure industry.

"I'm working for Professional Game Match Officials Ltd, run by the former referee Keith Hackett. It's a new scheme whereby former managers and players will be assessing referees, as well as every aspect of a Premier League fixture. We'll be getting to the ground two hours before kick-off and checking everything – the drug testing facilities, handing in of the team-sheets, talking to the police. Then afterwards we'll be part of the referee's de-briefing and submitting our report. It's been long overdue that referees work more closely with the other agencies involved in football." Few people are more ideally suited, or qualified.

Peter McParland

Mention to most Villa supporters that you've met a former player, and the response will range from mild curiosity to deep interest, depending on the level of their support and the fame of the player. Say that the man in question was Peter McParland, and their reaction is invariably akin to casually mentioning that you just popped up to Mount Sinai to have a word with Moses. The reason, of course, is that Peter remains the last Villa player to have scored in an FA Cup final victory, and almost half a century later you get the impression that when that record is finally broken, no-one will be happier than the winger from Newry, in Northern Ireland, who had been a supporter long before he made the journey over the Irish Sea to sign for the club.

Born in 1934, McParland grew up during the war with a father away working in Birmingham. "He used to send me the *Argus* over every week, so I was following the Villa from when I was a boy."

Leaving school at the age of fifteen, McParland found work as an apprentice coppersmith for the Great Northern Railways. However, he had already begun to make his mark as a footballer, playing for youth side Shamrock United, then Dundalk. The latter proved useful to his employment prospects as one of their directors was a big noise in the transport business and got the young McParland transferred to a less strenuous job at a bus garage. Such was the youngster's promise that a move to England was inevitable, and it came in 1952, immediately followed by an encouraging meeting with the then-Villa manager, George Martin.

Peter says of his arrival in Birmingham. "I got straight off the boat train at New Street, and there was George. He told me that I might be in the first team for the game that Saturday with Blackpool. They were one of the top teams in the country. Stanley Matthews was still with them, and I was worried that I wasn't ready.

In the end I played for the reserves, but on the Monday night I was in the first team against Wolves, who were another good side. We lost 1-0, and I wasn't picked for a year or so after that. I came into the team on Christmas Eve, 1953. Again it was against Wolves, at Molineux. I scored the only goal and I was always in the team from then on, unless I was injured."

McParland had fluctuated between wing-half and winger during his early days, and arguments raged throughout his career as to which was Peter's best position. His Villa colleague Danny Blanchflower regarded Peter as "the finest-ever British inside-forward," while eminent club historian Peter Morris thought of him as the club's best centre-forward since Pongo Waring, almost thirty years earlier, as well as the greatest Villa left-winger since Denny Hodgetts, who had achieved fame in the 1890s. His two goals in the 1957 FA Cup final, when Peter played on the wing, remain embedded in the memory of every Villa supporter who has seen them – either those lucky enough to have been at Wembley or anyone who has watched the video highlights. Yet he is also regarded as one of Northern Ireland's greatest-ever centre-forwards; a record of ten goals in 34 games standing up to the closest scrutiny, and his place in the 1958 World Cup finals, when he scored twice against West Germany, making him almost as much a legendary figure to Ulstermen as to Villa supporters.

The FA Cup triumph and victory in the inaugural League Cup four years later apart, Villa Park was rarely a happy place during McParland's time. Stagnation and decline was a way of life, and it seemed that neither a succession of managers nor the constant presence of an archaic board was able to change things. Eventually, after scoring 120 goals in 340 games, one of the greatest post-war Villa players departed to Wolves in January 1962 for a bargain fee of £30,000.

When asked about his premature departure from the club, Peter replies, "I fell out with Joe Mercer. I'd lost my trust in him; he never came to the point of what he wanted to say, so I thought it was about time I moved on. Some of the players told me to sit it out and see what transpired, but I wanted to move. I went from a manager who would never say anything to me straight out to Stan Cullis, who never minced his words. You knew where you stood with Stan."

However, McParland's time with Wolves was to be a short one. After playing a full part in the club's successful fight against relegation in his first season, Peter ran into problems before the following season had got underway. "We were out training the day before the first game, and I was playing with the ball when I tore a muscle. We beat Manchester City 8-1 in our opening match and got off to a good start, so I couldn't get into the team until things started going wrong."

McParland never fully regained his place in the Wolves side, playing just six more matches, and was soon on his way again despite another highly respectable tally of ten goals in 21 games. Several clubs were interested in signing McParland, but he decided to link up with former Villa colleague Alan O'Neill at Plymouth Argyle, then in the second division, in January 1963. "They were top of the table and I thought they were going places, but then we had that terrible winter in 1963 and we played just three matches in a couple of months. We lost two and drew the other and never got back on track afterwards. I stayed there for a couple of seasons, but I never really settled.

"We hadn't got rid of the house in Birmingham, so my wife moved back there and eventually I agreed to move to Worcester City, who were in the Southern League. Vic Crowe was coach of Peterborough and he asked me to play for him, but I'd already agreed to move to Worcester. Malcolm Allison joined Plymouth a few days after I left, and when I spoke to him he said that he'd have wanted to keep me and he could have got me playing as well as ever. I think he could have, and if I hadn't already gone when he became manager I'd probably have stayed with Plymouth."

Even though Peter's time with Plymouth had not been a great success, he still managed to score 14 goals in 38 games, eventually retiring from league football after having made over 400 senior appearances, averaging better than a goal every third game.

With McParland in the side, Worcester finished third in the Southern League twice in succession, but never looked like breaking into what was then the closed shop of the fourth division. He then decided to try his luck in the fledgling North American Soccer League. "Vic asked me to move with him to Atlanta Chiefs, in Georgia, so I moved over with my family in 1967. According to Phil

Woosnam, who was there with us, I was playing as well as ever and in my second year we won the All-American title. They made a big thing of it over there, that a city the size of Atlanta had never won anything in basketball American football or baseball, but they managed to be the soccer champions. I stayed in Atlanta until 1969, coaching and playing, but then things were looking a bit dicey with the league so we decided to come back home. My wife was all for returning to Britain, but looking back it was a bit of a mistake to return. Maybe we should have stayed there. We were due to go back for a reunion in the nineties, but the man who was organising it got a job with the involvement of the 1996 Olympics in Atlanta and it was forgotten."

Peter didn't stay in England for long, returning to his homeland, but with what turned out to be unfortunate timing, when he took the job of player/manager with Belfast-based Glentoran in 1969. "The Glens had a good record, particularly in Europe, but despite some quality players they weren't doing too well. I got them together and they said that one of the problems was that the press were getting on to them. I said 'Show them what you're made of,' and they responded." So much so that Glentoran won the league in 1969-70, which in itself meant that McParland's playing days were over. "They were a good side, so I let them get on with it" is his modest reflection on the end of a wonderful career.

Unfortunately, McParland's time with Glentoran was to coincide with the renewal of the troubles in Northern Ireland. "At first I went over there on my own. Then my family were going to come over, but the night before they were due to arrive, the shooting started in Belfast, so I told them to stay back in Birmingham. Then things started getting worse, and we were being warned that Catholics weren't welcome playing for us. My family had eventually moved over to Belfast, but one day when they were back in Birmingham on holiday it all started to get a lot worse and I told my wife to stay there. She didn't need much persuading, because not long before that she'd been looking in a shop window in Belfast and minutes later it was blown in when a bomb went off nearby."

However bad the situation might have been at this point, and it says a great deal for the Catholic McParland and his standing in Irish football that he was able to manage the Protestant Glentoran club with little problem, it was not without its humorous side. "Esso gave us £6,000, a lot of money in our position, to play Leeds, who were the English champions. I was at Windsor Park watching a game and one of the directors from Linfield, who were staunchly Protestant at the time, said that they'd better get some Catholics in the side if we were getting that kind of money to play friendlies. My assistant, Billy Neill, replied 'You've no chance. They'd get beaten up by the Prods because they're Catholic and by the Catholics because they're playing for a Protestant team. Anyway, they all want to play for us'."

Glentoran also had support from a useful source, albeit one which could have been even more productive had they but known. "Some years before I arrived, they'd been told about a young lad who lived close to the ground and his family were big Glens fans. He was dribbling rings round all the other kids at school, so the scout, Bud MacFarlane, went over to take a look at him. He came back and said 'His name's George Best and he's a great little player but he's too small.' George signed for Manchester United just after that, and his dad and his grandfather would sit behind me in the stand. They were forever shouting, telling me my job."

After leaving Glentoran, McParland moved to Cyprus as manager of Morphea. However, he soon became aware that a manager's job in the Cypriot league was not as straightforward as it might have been. "My time over there was okay, but there was plenty of match-fixing. One time we were playing Omonia – they were second in the league – and I heard something was going on. A couple of fellows who were friends of our committee men said that we could get £3,000 for throwing the match, and I got the feeling that the next thing they expected to hear from me was 'What's my cut?'

"I didn't want to know anything about it, and I told them as much. But it must have been well-known, because a supporter from Omonia turned up at my door with a large roll of banknotes and asked how much I needed to get my team to play along. I told him to put his money away because the game would be fair. Then, when we played, the score was 0-0 with five minutes to go when one of Omonia's midfielders started moving up. I could see what was going to happen, and I told one of my players to stand on him. Of course, he got loose in the last minute and scored the winner. I was furious in the dressing room, afterwards, because it looked so well rehearsed. And some years later the captain of my team told me that the game had been fixed."

From Cyprus, McParland moved to Kuwait, and another set of problems. "Alan Wade, who was at the FA, put me in contact with a team over there, Quadsia. They were a good side, seven of my players were in the Kuwaiti team that got to the World Cup finals in 1978, but one day I arrived at training and there were hardly any players there. I asked what had happened and was told that the missing ones were army reservists and Saddam Hussein had massed his troops near the border so they'd been called up. We used to get crowds of 20,000, and it'd be a strange sight as they were all wearing robes."

Football in the Gulf was, naturally, awash with money during the seventies and, as a result, some big names were encouraged to manage in the area. "Pat Saward, who played with me in 1957, was in Dubai, and left when Don Revie arrived. There were a few English managers in the Gulf; we set their football up then they decided they wanted Brazilian coaches so we started to leave."

Peter then moved into another strange situation. "I spent some time in Libya. Again, this had been set up by the F.A; they put me in contact with Afriki, who were bottom of the Libyan league. The club were in a desperate situation, but we put together a good run and eventually stayed up by winning the last game of the season. I'd been there for a couple of years, then I came home for Christmas and I heard that Colonel Gadaffi had banned football – no-one was allowed to play or watch, so that didn't leave much room for coaches. I was told I'd have my contract paid up and they'd get in touch if the situation changed. To their credit, the club got special clearance and I was sent the money from Libya."

His globe-trotting still not done, Peter then spent some time as coach to the Hong Kong national side ("They weren't much interested in football, and the league was crooked there as well"), before returning to Cyprus and creating a storm of controversy whilst managing A.E.L., of Limassol. "I told a newspaper reporter that the game was corrupt, and of course, my words were splashed across the back pages. I asked how one man, a multi-millionaire businessman who owned one of the clubs, could dance along the touchline when his team scored, knowing that the game was fixed. Naturally, it caused a furore. The Cypriot F.A. were angry, the Greek language newspapers gave me plenty of stick and my players said I'd end up in prison; but the club president received a phone call from the Minister of Sport who said 'If Mr McParland ends up in court, tell him I'll back him'. I'd had enough by then, so I resigned from A.E.L. and came back to Britain."

Since that time, Peter has spent his days in semi-retirement in Bournemouth, where he lives with his wife. "I did a bit of scouting; I play golf regularly, and my two sons live in Japan and Australia so I like to go and see them every couple of years." He makes regular trips to Villa Park, and can often be heard commentating on the club's Villan radio station.

To say, though, that Peter McParland is woven into the fabric of Aston Villa through his past deeds is only to tell part of the story. At a recent greyhound night, held at Perry Barr stadium in aid of the Former Players Association, queues formed at every table where those legendary figures were holding court. They signed autographs all night, and by far the longest queue was at the table where Peter McParland sat, with a word for everyone who sought his company. That amongst those willing to wait patiently in a queue for the great man's signature were Gary Shaw and Gordon Cowans says everything you need to know about him and his deeds.

But however long, illustrious and incident-packed his career may have been, Peter retains one more footballing ambition. "I want to see the Villa win the FA Cup again before I go," he says. And no matter how many Villa players may eventually write their names into the record books as trophy-winners, it's doubtful that any of them will retain the affection of the supporters more than Peter McParland.

Ian Ormondroyd

Bradford City's Valley Parade ground is testament to the way in which football clubs can rise above tribulation to become a shining example of modern thinking. Situated off the Manningham Lane area of the city, where Italian cafes rub shoulders with Caribbean takeaways and the ubiquitous Bradford curry houses, City have seen their fair share of turbulence. Administration in 2002 was the latest blow to a club whose darkest hour came when 56 supporters perished in the dreadful fire of May 1985. Bradford has also been a city oft-stricken by economic blight over the years and where political extremists of all persuasions have attempted to make capital out of the area's successive waves of immigrants. Which makes it an ideal place for a player often derided, yet at the same time still regarded with warm affection by Villa supporters.

Born in 1964, Ian Ormondroyd left school in Bradford to work for Grattan's, the mail order company who have for many years been one of the city's largest employers. "I did a bit of everything; warehouse, working in the shop, data input. Going from school into a real job stands you in good stead should you become a professional footballer later on. You realise how lucky you now are."

Playing in the local non-league scene, Ormondroyd was turning out for Thackley of the North-East Counties League, when, towards the end of the 1984-85 season, he came to the attention of the club he'd always supported. After a six-month trial, Ian signed professional forms at the beginning of the following season with City, newly-promoted to the old second division. At the same time they were struggling to come to terms with the aftermath of the fire, and forced to play their home games at the giant Odsal stadium.

Unsurprisingly, he was delighted, if not a little bewildered, at the turn of events. "As the saying goes, it was a dream come true to sign for the team I'd been following all my life. I'd been watching Bradford since I was young and my big idol had been Bobby Campbell, a centre-forward who'd started his career with the Villa. He was a great player but the kindest way you could describe him was to say he was crackers. He could have been a big star, Bobby, but he broke his leg and never really recovered."

Ormondroyd's time at Bradford was mostly a successful one as the club established themselves in the second division, making the play-offs in 1987-88, when a defeat at Villa Park towards the end of the season scuppered their chances of automatic promotion. "That was an amazing game. The ground was full; the noise was tremendous. You could see what a big club Villa were."

Indeed, it was Villa who were eventually promoted outright, while Bradford lost in the play-off semi-finals. The following season saw Graham Taylor pay what was then a club record of £650,000 to take Ormondroyd to Villa Park, after the player had scored 20 goals in 87 league appearances for his home-town club. Signed on the same day in February 1989 as the infuriatingly inconsistent Nigel Callaghan, Ormondroyd recalls: "I heard that Arsenal were in for me, which would have been interesting, but it was eventually Villa who I signed for. The two of us joined together, myself and Nigel. He was a strange character, wonderfully talented but with completely the wrong attitude. He could have been a great."

After making his Villa debut against Sheffield Wednesday, Ormondroyd's first few months at the club were not happy ones. The weight of his transfer hung heavy, not helped by a false report that the initial fee was due to be £65,000 and that Villa had inadvertently added an extra nought – a story which Graham Taylor has since denied. Form slumped and the team eventually avoided relegation thanks only to West Ham losing their final game, away at Liverpool, long after Villa had completed their fixtures. The following season saw a transformation, with the team finishing second in the league and Ormondroyd a revelation on the left side of midfield, where his height caused confusion amongst defenders who were regularly at odds over who should be marking the only 6 foot 4 inch winger in the first division.

Graham Taylor ("by a mile the best boss I ever worked for") departed to manage England and his unlikely replacement was the

Czech, Dr Josef Venglos. As with many of his contemporaries, Ormondroyd found the new boss's ideas somewhat strange. "He was unbelievable. He couldn't speak English and he had these foreign techniques that we couldn't understand. Stuff like drinking a certain amount of fluid on the morning of a game and then again at half-time. All I'd ever done was have a few sips of tea during the interval, but he had everything measured out. And drinking alcohol; I used to have the odd beer, and Jo wanted us to cut it out completely. He was keen on sorting our diets out, getting the right balance of proteins and carbohydrates. We used to take no notice, but of course, everyone now does what Jo was trying to get us to do."

The highlight of the 1990-91 season was Villa's two-legged UEFA Cup tie versus Inter. After a memorable 2-0 victory at Villa Park, the team were beaten 3-0 away from home, with Ormondroyd a substitute. He remembers the evening vividly. "We went out on to the pitch an hour before kick-off, and we had to go underground, as though we were going through a car park. Then suddenly we were out on to the pitch, and even that early there were 50,000 in there, throwing firecrackers and flares and making a hell of a noise. It was very intimidating.

"We got off to a poor start, letting in an early goal, and then Tony Cascarino missed that chance and we ended up losing 3-0. It was a disappointment, and we never really recovered, but it was still a wonderful experience."

With Villa once more holding on to first division status by the skin of their teeth, Venglos was replaced by Ron Atkinson. Ormondroyd retains positive, if brief, memories of the most colourful character English management has seen for many years. "I liked him, and we got on okay. He said to me almost straight away that I wasn't part of his plans, which was honest of him, and I joined Derby in the September of 1991, just after the season had started."

Ormondroyd had scored 10 goals in 56 games with Villa, and Derby paid £400,000 as part of what was intended to be a promotion push to the first division. However, he was to spend less than six months at the ramshackle Baseball Ground. "It was a lot different from Villa Park. You have to say that the ground wasn't the best, in fact in many ways it was awful, but with the spectators so close to the pitch it made for a great atmosphere."

Arthur Cox was in charge – another manager of whom Ormondroyd retains fond memories. "He was an old-fashioned boss. A good motivator, he made training fun. I was doing well, as we were on the fringes of the promotion race all the time I was there."

However much Ormondroyd was enjoying himself at Derby, though, his time there was to prove a short one. By March 1992, after just 25 games and eight goals, he was making the short trip to Leicester. There Ian would join another promotion push, but this one boasted a claret and blue tinge. "Derby's chairman, Lionel Pickering, was spending a lot of money and he wanted Paul Kitson of Leicester, who was tipped as the next big thing. Brian Little, the Leicester manager, said he would only let Kitson go if he could have me, Paul Gee and a lot of money in exchange. I was happy at Derby and I didn't want to move, but Arthur made it clear that if I didn't sign for Leicester then I wouldn't be part of his plans, so I was off again."

With Little as his manager and a backroom staff including Allan Evans and John Gregory, Ormondroyd enjoyed three fruitful years at Leicester as the club seemingly struggled against promotion to the newly-created Premier League. "We got to three play-off finals and I was involved in all of them. Brian was a great manager and we got on well, although he sometimes tried to back down from confrontation. He wouldn't tell players if they'd been dropped, he'd write the team on a blackboard and let the players come into the dressing room on the day of the game. If your name was on the board you were in the team.

"He would often take the forwards for training and then we could see what a marvellous talent he had. He'd had some trouble with his back, and very often after he'd been showing us some of his tricks he'd hobble off the pitch and say 'I shouldn't be doing this'."

It did seem for a while as though Little was fated never to attain promotion. Leicester first got to the play-off final in 1992, when they met Blackburn, heavily financed in their attempts to get to the Premier League by the first of Jack Walker's handouts. "George Courtney was the referee and it was his last match before retiring. Brian said to us before the game 'He'll give a penalty today, he'll want a bit of controversy.' And he did. David Speedie scored it and that was enough to keep us down. The following season we had a marvellous match with Swindon, when I came on as sub. We were three down, pulled it back to 3-3, then Steve White scored late on. And finally, 1995, which made up for the two other disappointments. We beat Derby, and it was probably our worst performance of the lot. Tommy Johnson had about four one-on-ones for them and missed them all; our keeper Kevin Poole made some great saves and we sneaked a goal towards the end."

Back in the top flight, Ormondroyd found himself the victim of management upheaval as Little fulfiled his destiny to become Villa manager, amongst much controversy, in November 1994 and was replaced at Filbert Street by Mark McGhee. For Ormondroyd, this was the end of his career in the top division. "McGhee and I didn't get on. I went out on loan to Hull, who were then in the second division, did okay there and got six goals in ten games. Then the manager called me back, played me in one game, against Wimbledon, and after that I never got near the first team again."

The inevitable transfer took place during the summer of 1995, with Ormondroyd, after 77 games for Leicester that had seen him score seven goals, returning home to Bradford for £175,000. "They were back in what was then the second division, but I wasn't worried about going back, or dropping down a couple of divisions. We did well and got to the play-off finals, after an amazing turnaround against Blackpool. We lost 2-0 at home, and beat them 3-0 up there, although I can't claim much credit because I wasn't in the team for the return. I came back for the final, which we lost to Notts County. Lennie Lawrence was the manager, then, when he left, Chris Kamara got the job."

By now Ormondroyd was beginning to suffer with injuries, and was restricted to just 38 games in a season and a half, during which time he scored six goals, before moving to Oldham, themselves struggling in the second division. He does not, however, retain any great fondness for his time at Boundary Park.

"Graeme Sharp was the manager, and he wasn't the best. He couldn't really inspire players, despite what he'd done as a player himself, although his assistant, Colin Harvey, did a good job. I was there for just over a season, then I dropped down into the third to play for Scunthorpe."

Ormondroyd is honest enough to admit that his time playing in one of football's outposts wasn't the best way to finish a long and often successful career. "I shouldn't have gone there. I was having to rely on tablets to get me through games. I said to the manager, Brian Laws, before I signed 'My left ankle's gone and my right one isn't up to much', and he said that was fair enough and I should do whatever I could. The supporters, though, didn't understand. They pay their money and they don't see things like that. They probably just saw a player who'd spent most of his career in the top couple of divisions and thought I was being paid a lot of money, which I wasn't, unfortunately. It certainly wasn't a last big payday. "

Goalless in twenty games with the club, Ormondroyd can look back on his time at Scunthorpe with some amusement. "In 2005 the fans voted me their worst player ever. That's really something, isn't it? To be the worst player Scunthorpe have ever had."

Retiring from football at the end of the 1997-98 season, Ian found the usual ex-professional problem of adjusting to life out of work, before reaching salvation amongst familiar surroundings. "Bradford had been running a Football In The Community scheme since 1989. They needed someone to manage it and I was offered the job."

Ormondroyd's return coincided with the most successful period of Bradford's modern history, culminating in promotion to the Premier League in 1999. However, there was to be a sting in this particular fairy tale. "The first season was great. Everyone treated it as a holiday, enjoyed themselves and didn't go overboard. Then the money started to flow in, and the people in charge thought that the good times would last forever."

Indeed, chairman Geoffrey Richmond embarked on what he famously called "fifteen minutes of madness" during the summer of 2000, in an attempt to consolidate Bradford's position at the elite level of English football. Ormondroyd recalls the time when his club attempted to compete with the elite. "We signed big name players on big money and forgot everything that had brought success in the first place. Seven or eight players came in on ridiculous money. Benito Carbone was signed; he was on about £40,000 a week and he did nothing. He was the sort of player who would look great and you'd think he was wonderful when he was doing those flicks and bringing the ball down at thigh-height just killing it stone dead. Then you'd realise that he was doing all this stuff fifty yards out where he wasn't being marked. He didn't want to know in the danger zone. Dan Petrescu, Lee Sharpe, they were another couple of big money signings who did nothing. And of course, Stan Collymore. He was amazing – he'd drive into the car park, stick his car where he wanted and walk away, blocking a load of cars in. That was typical of Stan. He never thought about anyone else."

The result was inevitable. Although Richmond's spending of money that they never possessed was no more than several other clubs were doing, Bradford's relegation back to the first division in 2001, coupled with the collapse of the ITV digital TV deal the following year, spelt financial trouble for the club, who entered into administration. Although the Football in the Community scheme is a separate entity from the football side, times were still difficult. "Luckily, we're self-funding, so the scheme was never in jeopardy, but it was still a difficult period. The general feeling was that City were going out of business, and this was reflected in the low numbers we could attract on to our courses. It seemed that there were very few people who wanted to be associated with a club that was in trouble."

But City survived, thanks to help from their Supporters' Trust and a new chairman, local businessman Julian Rhodes, of whom Ormondroyd says, "He did a magnificent job. Without him, Bradford would have gone out of business." As with many other clubs struggling to survive in the shadow of bigger neighbours, life remains difficult, and Football in the Community helps to bring the club closer to the local population. Ian explains his role in the scheme: "My job is to encourage young people to play and watch football. We run after-school clubs, get them along to the games and do penalty shoot-outs on the pitch, that sort of thing. It's difficult to get youngsters to realise that there's a football club in their area when so many of them want to support Leeds or Manchester United, but that's the job I have to do. Ironically, and I know it might sound bad, but the aftermath of the fire made my job easier in that respect. There's still a strong bond between the club and supporters because of what happened, in much the same way as Liverpool experienced with their fans after Hillsborough."

Life in a rundown, multi-racial area such as Bradford can present other problems than persuading potential football supporters that there is life outside the Premiership. "Of course Asian kids are interested on football, but we appreciate that there are certain religious considerations which might hamper them playing and watching. We also realise that Bradford and the surrounding area is not a well-off place and going to the match can be an expensive hobby. We're in the process of appointing a local Cohesion Officer to help in that and other respects, and we attempt to emphasise that any decent player will be invited to try out for our School of Excellence regardless of their background."

We were speaking shortly after Peter Crouch became one of the most unlikely-ever England internationals. As someone whose appearance caused obvious comparisons with another former Villa forward, Ormondroyd was, naturally, sympathetic to some of the problems Crouch has faced. "The staff here reckon he's my love child," he jokes. "Peter's done well; he's a different player to me, a more natural goal scorer, and it's good that people are looking past his appearance.

"I felt for him when he first joined Villa. The team were playing badly, and he was a natural target. I had the same, and continued to get some stick even when we were doing well. Tony Daley would beat a player and hit a cross into the Holte End but they loved him for it. I'd do the same and get booed."

Despite never having been accepted by some sections of the crowd, even though most still remember him with warmth, Ormondroyd looks back on his time at Villa Park, and the rest of his professional career, fondly, although he does have one regret. "If we'd won that game at home to Wimbledon in 1990, when we were top of the table and David Platt missed the penalty early on, we'd have won the league.

"Maybe we just weren't good enough in the end, but we finished second, although it would have been nice to have a medal, some sort of recognition for how well the team did. I'm not too worried, though. I played at Wembley half a dozen times and I was involved in a few play-offs. If I'd been around five or six years later I'd have been a rich man now, but I can't complain. I played professionally for fourteen years and I enjoyed it."

Living near Bradford and married with two boys, Ian recalls how his then-fiancé would watch him at Villa Park in circumstances far removed from the world of Footballers' Wives. "She was a police officer, and transferred to the West Midlands when I joined Villa. There were a few times when she was on duty at the ground while I was playing, but she didn't arrest anyone for badmouthing me."

Many players keep in touch once their playing days are over, but Ormondroyd has resisted the temptation. "I went down to Paul Birch's 40th birthday party a couple of years ago, and that was an enjoyable night, but none of us has much in common now. I saw David Platt at Valley Parade as well, when he was England under-21s manager. He didn't speak."

Mark Walters

I found the sight of Mark Walters making his debut one of the most depressing moments of my life. Not that there was anything wrong with his performance, but rather that Walters was the first Villa player born after I was. No longer could I kid myself that I was a late developer; the truth had to be faced. I was never going to be spotted during a Sunday morning kickabout and whisked off to Bodymoor Heath to train with the European Champions-elect. The closest I was ever going to get to any of those heroes was by sitting across a table and asking the cause of my late-teens depression about his career.

Born in Aston in 1964, Walters' debut came during the second half of a 4-1 home defeat to Leeds United in April 1982, at the age of 17. It was typical of that upside-down season that Villa would two months later win the European Cup, while Leeds would be relegated to the old second division.

Walters had been tipped for stardom at an early age. Brian Little, fighting a losing battle against the knee problems that would force him into a premature retirement, was witnessing from the sidelines as Walters made his way through the Villa's junior sides, and later remarked. "Mark was the best player I ever saw at that age."

Early signs were encouraging as Walters became a fixture in the Villa team that was steadily declining from its 1982 peak, also playing nine times for the England under-21 side to add to his youth and schoolboy representative honours. By the time Graham Taylor became manager five years later, Villa had been relegated and the out of contract Walters wanted away, his explanation echoing the reasons David O'Leary gave for selling Darius Vassell, another local lad who became an England international, at the end of the 2004-05 season. "Playing for Villa had become too comfortable for me. I could have stayed there forever and had an easy life, but the club seemed to have no ambition. They'd just gone down and I wanted to get away. I'd been born in Aston, played for Villa since I left school, and I wanted to broaden my horizons. If I'd known how things would turn out under Graham Taylor I might have stayed, but that's with the benefit of hindsight, and you can't have everything. Graham was great for me, though. He taught me so much about what you have to do both physically and mentally to be a top-class player. I wish I'd have known him longer."

Walters stayed with Villa until Christmas of 1987, in total playing 200 games and scoring 47 goals. By the time he left, the team had recovered from an uncertain start and were looking good for promotion back to the first division, which they eventually achieved by the slimmest-possible margin the following May. By this time, Walters had moved into an entirely different world after a £615,000 move to Scottish giants, Rangers. The Glasgow club were then the talk of British football, after a takeover by the wealthy Lawrence Marlborough had seen them install Graeme Souness as manager and embark upon a spending spree unprecedented in the history of the Scottish league. Walters was just one of a number of arrivals from south of the border who included England captain Terry Butcher and his fellow internationals Chris Woods, Graham Roberts and Trevor Francis. The opportunity of playing alongside such big names was a key factor in Walters' decision to become the first high-profile black player to sign for a Scottish club.

"It was strictly a career move. I'd fancied going south, and it would have taken a lot for me to go three hundred miles the other way, but everything at Rangers seemed right. They offered almost guaranteed European football, at a time when English clubs were still banned, and they were winning trophies regularly."

As if joining Rangers wasn't enough, Walters was due to make his debut in the unique atmosphere of an Old Firm, New Year derby. What followed on 2nd January 1988 was one of the most shameful moments in the history of Scottish football. Veteran TV commentator Archie McPherson began his report of the match later that night by saying, "What happened here today makes me ashamed to be Scottish." Walters was showered with bananas by Celtic supporters, and then had to endure much the same treatment during his next game, away at Hearts. He says of his arrival in Scotland, "I was playing in the biggest goldfish bowl around. Rangers were the Chelsea of their day, spending money and dominating football. I was the biggest focal point, and I knew what I was in for right from the start. There was all the publicity about the game; on the morning I was watching TV and this Celtic fan was standing in front of a fruit stall saying 'This is what Walters is going to get'. When the match was on I had all sorts chucked at me, fruit, pigs feet, darts, the lot. If I'd picked them up I wouldn't have had to buy any food for a month. It was worse at Hearts, though. Tynecastle is a much smaller ground than Parkhead and the pitch is closer to the stand so, whereas the Celtic supporters couldn't get their missiles anywhere near me, at Hearts things were flying over my head. I tried to remain focused on the game, but it was hard."

Rangers supporters, whose loyalist history often sees them accused of flirting with the far-right, were hardly innocents themselves at this point, but Walters' arrival played a major part in breaking down the barriers which still existed in Scottish football. The Rangers fanzine *Follow, Follow* featured a picture of the player on its front cover under the heading 'Blue – The Only Colour That Matters', and the club's supporters regularly made their feelings known at Ibrox. "On one occasion someone shouted a racist remark, and it was his own supporters who threw him out before the police could get there," recalls Mark.

Walters' first season in Scotland saw Rangers finish a disappointing third in the Scottish Premier League, but under the chairmanship of multi-millionaire businessman David Murray, who took the club over in November 1988, their wealth saw them win the Scottish title nine times in a row. Walters was one of the key figures in the first three of these triumphs. "It was like being a pop star. I had a taste of what players nowadays must get. If I drank I'd have been paralytic most of the time because I never had to pay for anything. Whenever we went out there was always someone who wanted to pay for the players."

Life for an Old Firm footballer off the field is always trying. Had Walters been the type of player who enjoyed an active social life he may well have gone the way of many other great talents that have been wasted in the Scottish game. Fortunately, good sense prevailed, as he explains. "It was a bit like being under surveillance 24 hours a day. But I was lucky in that I always went to places that had been recommended to me. Bars, restaurants that kind of thing, where I was told there wouldn't be any problems. Some of the players in the team got into a bit of trouble, but it was usually when they were being provoked. Most of the time they were able to walk away.

"I had a great time in Glasgow, I loved the place then and I still do. David Murray, who had become chairman soon after I arrived, was a great man. He gave me some good advice and we're still close friends. He gets some stick from the fans for the way he runs the club, but it's his business and his money at stake. It's easy to gamble with someone else's money, but how many of the supporters who say that he, or Doug Ellis for that matter, should spend more would put their own money at risk?"

Rangers won consecutive titles from 1989-91, however, the third of these was won in difficult circumstances following the departure of manager Graeme Souness to Liverpool in March 1991. "It was a big shock," says Walters. "But maybe he thought he'd gone as far as he could with Rangers and he wanted a fresh challenge." One of the problems facing Souness was Europe, as despite regular European Cup appearances, the team failed time and again to compete with the big guns on the continent. Walters believes that this was down to the way in which Scottish teams had adapted their own style of play to cope with Rangers' superior manpower. "We'd be playing a team like Kilmarnock, who'd have ten men behind the ball even at home, then four days later we'd be up against Bayern Munich. It was hardly ideal preparation."

During the summer of 1991, Walters made what was to prove his only appearance for the full England side, against New Zealand under the managership of Graham Taylor. He also embarked upon the second big-money move of his career, when he became one of Graeme Souness's first signings for Liverpool. Walters was by now 27 years old, and had made 106 league appearances for Rangers, scoring 32 goals, as well as making an appearance for the England 'B' team against Wales, in February 1991. His legacy to Scottish football, though, can never be understated.

Walters was the first high-profile black player to arrive in the country, and he played for a club whose supporters have often been singled out as the standard bearers of intolerance and bigotry. Not only did they accept the presence of Mark Walters in their team, but he remains a favourite amongst the Ibrox faithful to this day. When the Rangers Supporters Trust was formed in 2003, Walters was at their inaugural meeting and invited to become the group's first honorary member. However, this was an honour that he felt unable to accept. "I was flattered to be recognised in such a way, but I was advised to turn it down, because of the political implications. I remain good friends with David Murray, and being associated with the Trust might have caused some embarrassment."

Walters' time at Liverpool was not the great success he would have hoped. The team was in decline from its glory years and supporters weren't happy when pictures of Graeme Souness, celebrating from his hospital bed when Liverpool made it through to the 1992 Cup Final, appeared in the *Sun*, whose coverage of the Hillsborough disaster still burned deep into the Merseyside psyche. Why Souness should choose to get involved with the paper, knowing what the reaction would be from Liverpool fans, is still unknown. Walters is unable to shed any light on the subject. "I don't know why he did it. It was insensitive, and it caused a few problems, but as a player I didn't get too concerned."

Liverpool's FA Cup triumph over second division Sunderland was the high-spot of Walters' four years on Merseyside. It came, though, during a bad personal time for the player.

"My wife gave birth to a stillborn child, and that had a big effect on me. I didn't take much notice of what was going on around me. Souness was trying to replace some old favourites and maybe he did it too soon. It's difficult to know when to break up a successful squad; Walter Smith couldn't do it at Rangers after I left, but Arsene Wenger had the right idea. He knew when the best time was to let players go as they were coming to the end of their peak years.

"I had a difficult time at Anfield. John Barnes was still there and Steve MacManaman was doing well. I'd been seen as the replacement for Barnes and for various reasons that had never happened. I had a few highlights – the cup final when I was a substitute was a great day, and there was the game earlier that season when I scored the winner against Manchester United to deny them the title. I was so pleased with that goal and what it meant to the supporters that I ended up dancing with the corner flag in front of the Kop."

The cup triumph apart, Souness' time at Anfield was not a successful one and many of his signings fell short of the standards expected by supporters who had been used to almost constant triumphs over the previous two decades. Walters offers an explanation as to why Liverpool found success hard to come by during this period. "The fans thought they had a divine right to success, so they criticised almost all the players, who in their eyes weren't good enough. They didn't realise that nothing lasts forever. If you're at a big club, though, you have to take that. I didn't let them get to me. I thought that I could play, and that was what mattered."

Souness was eventually sacked by Liverpool after an embarrassing FA Cup defeat to Bristol City in January 1994. His successor, former Liverpool player Roy Evans, sent Walters out on loan to Stoke City, where he played nine games, scoring twice, and then to Wolves, where the player was to link up once more with Graham Taylor for 11 matches in which he scored three goals. Of this frustrating time, Mark says, "I hadn't lost any of my respect for Graham, even though he was going through a hard time at Wolves. He was a great manager and remains a great man, one of the few honest men in a dishonest industry. I still use him as a reference on job applications."

Walters was to win a Coca-Cola Cup winners medal for Liverpool, as a substitute against Bolton in 1995, but his career at Anfield was ending and he left for Southampton in January 1996. In total he made 115 full appearances for Liverpool, and scored 19 goals. "Roy Evans wanted me to stay, but I was hardly getting a game and at that stage of my career I wanted to be playing regularly."

Walters moved to Southampton, but stayed on the south coast for just five months, playing six games, before moving on at the end of the season. He still recalls this short spell vividly, although the anger has given way to some amusement. "I didn't get on with the manager, what was his name again? Merrick? No, that was the Elephant Man. Dave Merrington, that was it. Not much difference. I don't think he liked the fact that I was a big name and I'd played for some top clubs. One of his favourite phrases to me was 'You wouldn't win egg cups playing like that', and one time I answered back 'Maybe not, but I've already won a few'. I never answered a manager back usually, but I did to him."

Walters moved to Swindon, who were then in the second division and struggling to regroup after a brief sojourn into the Premier League and the loss of manger Glenn Hoddle. "By now I was playing for fun. All the worries about how my career was going were over and I was enjoying myself. The crowds weren't massive, but they were on my side. When I arrived I was worried that they might have thought I was there to earn a last payday and do as little as possible, but they never gave that impression, and neither did I do anything to make them think that was the case."

Walters played 112 league games in four seasons with Swindon, the longest he had stayed at one club since his Villa Park days, and scored 25 goals. He ended his time at the County Ground as a player-coach, and, when he moved to Swindon's close rivals Bristol Rovers during the 1999-2000 season, was able to continue with this side of the game. "Again, I enjoyed myself. Rovers were in the bottom divisions, but I was playing for enjoyment. I started off coaching the youth team, then the reserves. I'd been there for two years when Ray Graydon became manager. I could have stayed, but it was obvious that he wanted his own men around him, and he also had to cut the wage bill. I was 37 by then; I'd had a good career, so I agreed to leave."

Walters played 82 league games for Rovers, scoring an impressive 25 goals. He had also found time during the summer of 2001 to fly out to South Africa, taking part in a charity game with an FA invitational side to raise funds for the victims of the disaster at Ellis Park in Johannesburg where 43 people had been killed during a game two months previous.

However, leaving Rovers was not to be the end of Mark's playing career. He moved into non-league football, in addition to working as a coach at the Villa Academy. "I knew the manager of Ilkeston, and I said to him 'I'll play for you on Saturdays, but I can't train'. This lasted for about four months, then things got difficult."

Walters then did the rounds of several junior sides in the West Midlands, where his presence was sufficient to add a few extra spectators to the gate as well as bringing out the best in team-mates and opponents alike. Of this enjoyable finale to his career, Mark says, "My marriage had broken up, and I had no reason to pack in playing. I was enjoying myself, even if the conditions weren't always what I'd been used to. I played a few matches for Tividale, but I didn't enjoy it very much there. They've got one hell of a slope on that pitch and about two dozen supporters. I signed for Willenhall, in the Doc Marten's League. That must be the coldest ground in the country. Finally, I was with Dudley Town, who are in the West Midlands League. I had a good time with them, but by now I was finding it difficult to fit playing around my coaching commitments, so I packed in at the end of the 2004-05 season. That's it; I've retired now, except for some Old Stars games. I play for Liverpool and Rangers, but unfortunately Villa usually play their matches on Sundays, so I can't get to them. That's it for my footballing, unless someone makes it worth my while to start again."

Walters' coaching expertise has seen him forsake the uncertain life of trying to climb the management ladder in club football for a steadier life of working both with the Villa Academy, and on his own. "I got involved with a company called Premier Soccer Schools through a contact I made at Swindon, and I travel the world coaching youngsters. I've just been to Canada, Hong Kong and Thailand, and I'm off to the USA soon. It keeps me busy and out of mischief."

Now divorced and living in Solihull, with a son and a daughter, Mark Walters' life hasn't exactly panned out the way he expected, not that he's complaining. He explains, "When I was married I'd always banked on retiring when I was 35. Then when I got there I was single again, so I carried on playing. I don't do much planning ahead now. I believe that what's going to happen will happen, and I'm happy with what I've got. You can only live in one house and drive one car at a time. My family are fine, I'm secure and I wouldn't swap what I've done for anything else."

Walters adds, "I could have stayed at Villa for all my career, but if I hadn't moved I wouldn't have had that great experience at Rangers. Then, I could have stayed at Ibrox. They won the title six years in a row after I left, and I would have been in most of those teams. But if I'd done that I wouldn't have seen what it was like to play for Liverpool and I wouldn't have picked up the medals I won there. I've been in football for 25 years, played hundreds of games and I've got no regrets."

UP FRONT

Tony Cascarino

It would be fair to say that Tony Cascarino will never dine out on the strength of his Villa Park playing career. He was at the club for just over a season, during which time Graham Taylor's first side ended their ultimately unsuccessful challenge for the league title, and he then experienced their rapid decline under Josef Venglos. However, Cascarino's story after his departure from the club is as fascinating as that of any player who enjoyed a far more illustrious career in claret and blue.

We met at a French-themed bar in the quintessentially English village of Chislehurst, which is as good a place as any to talk to the English-born son of an Italian father, and played for the Republic of Ireland, even if his eligibility for such an honour was later questioned. Born in Orpington, Kent, in September 1962, Cascarino had an unorthodox start to his football career. "I left school at 16 and started working as a builder, doing work on the Thames Flood Barrier in London. It was long hours – we'd be doing eleven or twelve hours a day so football was out, but the money was good. Then my mother got me a job as a hairdresser's apprentice. I went from £150 a week in my hand to £22, but the people I was working with were a lot better looking."

Working more sociable hours allowed Cascarino to sign for local side Crockenhill, of the Kent League. Even here, though, things were not as they might have been. "I played for six months at centre-half, then I got pushed up front after our centre-forward broke his leg. We were due to play Erith & Belvedere, and I was driving to the match when I saw this nice looking girl on the pavement. She, er, distracted my attention and I ended up crashing the car. It was a write-off. I had to walk a mile to the ground, and when I got there I scored a hat-trick." Were this a Mills & Boon, the story would have ended with Cascarino meeting the girl later that night and wedding bells ensuing. Instead, "I didn't have a clue who she was. I never saw here again."

Romantic distractions aside, so well did Cascarino play for Crockenhill that he attracted the attention of third division Gillingham, for whom he signed professional forms in January 1982. The transfer fee was, as you might expect, an unorthodox one, and has since then repeatedly returned to haunt the player. "They gave Crockenhill a set of tracksuits, some training equipment, that sort of thing. It was a goodwill gesture, and Crockenhill were grateful, but I've never lived down the fact that I was swapped for a set of tracksuits."

Cascarino spent six years with Gillingham, scoring 78 goals in 219 league appearances and making the first of his appearances for the Republic of Ireland, before a £225,000 move to Millwall in August 1987. It was at Cold Blow Lane that he first made his name, playing for the South London side as they won the second division title in 1988, securing promotion to the top flight for the only time in their history. Cascarino formed a deadly partnership with Teddy Sherringham, and his 128 games for Millwall saw him netting 49 goals prior to a £1.5 million move to Villa in March 1990.

Cascarino's transfer, which shattered Villa's record fee of £650,000 paid for Ian Ormondroyd the previous year, has since been shrouded in controversy. It has been claimed that Villa really wanted Sherringham, and Graham Taylor bought the wrong player. Taylor himself has stated that he was, indeed, interested in Cascarino's partner but, once Millwall chairman Reg Burr had refused to sanction such a deal, Doug Ellis arranged the purchase of Cascarino, at a fee Taylor himself believed to be inflated in order to prevent the club from paying a large amount of corporation tax which would otherwise have been due. It is also reckoned that the signing of Cascarino cost Villa the title, as the style of play that had been so effective up until that point had to be altered, and the team suffered as a result. However, it has to be born in mind that the team had lost three of its previous four games prior to Cascarino's arrival, without scoring in any of them.

Villa's title challenge fell away and Cascarino failed to score until the final home game of the season, a 3-3 draw with Norwich, by which time the league title was as good as lost. However, had things been different in his debut, away at Derby, this chapter, and the rest of Tony Cascarino's life, may have been completely different. "I met a cross from fifteen yards out, and hit a perfect header. How Peter Shilton got to it, I'll never know – probably because he was the best keeper in the world. If that had gone in things may have been different, but I'm not sure."

Taylor departed for England duty after Italia '90, in which Cascarino had played a full part in Ireland's eventual run to the quarter-finals. That his club manager replaced Bobby Robson as England boss was a matter of regret for Aston Villa in general and for Tony Cascarino in particular. In common with most players who came under Taylor's management, even for a brief period, Cascarino has nothing but admiration for the man. "When Graham left, that was a major blow. I needed hard training and Graham's was the best I ever came across."

The arrival of Josef Venglos led to a dramatic change in the way the playing side of the club was run, and in common with many of his team-mates, Cascarino was unimpressed at the time with the Czech coach's methods. "The place became a Christmas club. Jo was a lovely man, but he had a real problem with one or two players. David Platt, for example, had come back from the World Cup a big star and he just wasn't interested. He wanted a move, and he didn't care about the team as long as he was doing well. Gordon Cowans was doing his running for him. Platt just wanted to be getting the goals. Overnight, the team ethic that had stood us in good stead went out of the window, we lost everything that we were about."

However, the time with Villa had helped Cascarino to further make the acquaintance of someone with whom he would spend plenty of time even after he had left the club, namely his Irish international colleague, Paul McGrath. "We roomed together at Villa and when we were playing for the Republic. Paul had a great effect on me; he showed what a great player could be like. I've seen some things in football, and what some players get up to before a game, but Paul was at a level far above anything that I'd imagined before. And he could play like nothing on earth."

Cascarino, though, has rather different words to say about another former Republic team-mate, David O'Leary. "I never thought he'd become a manager. In all the time that we played together, he never mentioned football. He'd tell you plenty about himself, you'd know what kind of hi-fi equipment he owned or how many cars he drove, but you'd never, for example, find out if he preferred playing with three or four at the back, how he liked the game played, which players he rated. He didn't seem that interested in football."

With Venglos having gone after a season which saw Villa make a promising start but decline alarmingly and narrowly avoid relegation, Ron Atkinson rolled into town, and Cascarino's time at Villa Park was almost at an end. "I'd got back for pre-season training early, then played in a five-a-side. I had a disaster and Ron was watching. He made his mind up about me there and then, and to his credit he was totally up-front about it. He told me that he didn't fancy me and I could move if I wanted. We can both laugh about it now, but, credit to him, he was honest. There was no bullshit involved."

A £1.1 million offer from Celtic in July 1991 saw Cascarino's time at Villa come to an end after 50 games and 12 goals. It was hardly a glittering career but, in the player's defence, he was signed when the team was running out of steam, and the following season had been a struggle for all concerned.

However disappointing the his Villa career had been, playing for Celtic quickly became a nightmare. Rangers were dominating Scottish football and their bitter Glaswegian rivals, by comparison, were in deep trouble. Celtic's board had become a by-word for incompetence and financial mis-management and to make matters worse, the Taylor Report had recommended that major British football grounds should become all-seater. Celtic, whose Parkhead ground held more terrace places than any other stadium in the country, were unsure whether to upgrade their antiquated home or move to a new stadium and while the club's owners dithered, Rangers moved further ahead. Liam Brady, Celtic manager at the time, brought in Cascarino at a club record fee in the hope that the player would be able to make much the same impact as had Mark Hateley for Rangers.

In hindsight, Cascarino's career in Scotland was doomed from the outset, a point he readily concedes. "I should never have gone there. I didn't enjoy Glasgow at all; everyone wanted a piece of me, and I got stick everywhere I went."

The time was not, though, without its humorous side, regardless of how unintentionally the situation may have arisen. "I went into a bookies one day after training. I was wearing my tracksuit and I got a few strange looks, but I didn't think much to it. The next day I mentioned to the players where I'd been and they looked at me in horror. It turned out that I'd been to Bridgeton, which is the biggest Rangers stronghold in Glasgow." Indeed, it's one of the ironies of Glaswegian life that Rangers' heartland area is less than a mile from Parkhead, and it's not overstating the case to say that anyone remotely linked with Celtic would, even now, be lucky to escape from the area unscathed.

Journalist Kevin McCarra, who saw much of Cascarino's time at Parkhead, says, "Tony was brought in by Liam Brady, presumably because of the Irish link. Having him in the team caused their style of play to change – he was a target man and they would lump the ball up to him, which didn't fit in with the Celtic traditions. Rangers were at their height, they were spending massive amounts on players while Brady was bringing in the likes of Stuart Slater and Gary Gillespie, who didn't come off, and supporters were getting restless. For a player who was always short of self-confidence, like Tony, Celtic in the early nineties was the worst club in the world to move to."

Cascarino was at Celtic for just seven months, during which time he played 40 games and scored 4 goals, although one of these strikes, at least, brought some credit as it was the equaliser in a 1-1 draw with Rangers. Brady had quickly realised that Cascarino's strengths were incompatible with his team-mates and the striker found himself the subject of a third big money move in less than three years – a straight swap for Chelsea's Tommy Boyd seeing both players valued at £750,000 in February 1992.

For the player, a move back to England could not be completed quickly enough. "Andy Townsend sold Chelsea to me. He was their captain and he persuaded me to move, not that I needed much talking into getting away from Celtic. When Tommy was thinking over his move, I was praying that there wouldn't be a problem. Celtic were the only club that I had no regrets about leaving. I'd been sad to leave Gillingham and Millwall, they were lovely, family clubs. I was gutted to move from Villa – they might have been a big club, but they still had that family atmosphere where everyone seemed to know everyone else."

It's worth remembering the state of play at Stamford Bridge during what was to prove the final season of the old first division, before a succession of wealthy tycoons brought success to a hitherto middling club. "Ian Porterfield was manager, and there was an amazing array of characters at the club. Vinnie Jones, Dennis Wise, Kerry Dixon, people like that. Training, though, was a joke. The manager would try to get us to do some running, and they'd swear at him and start playing five-a-sides. Andy Townsend would roll up half an hour late and say the traffic was bad – nearly every day. It wasn't very professional, but it helped me to enjoy my football a lot more after the time at Celtic." Scoring on his debut in a 1-1 draw with Crystal Palace helped boost Tony's always-frail confidence, but he would net just once more before the season ended.

The summer of 1992 saw Cascarino undergo knee surgery, and he was missing for much of the following season. Unsurprisingly, given his relationship with his playing staff, Porterfield didn't last long in the manager's role and his short-term replacement, former Chelsea player David Webb, took over in February 1993. "Tough as old boots," was the Cascarino verdict. "He stood no nonsense and his training was extremely hard."

Webb's time at Chelsea was over in a matter of months, and the next man into the Stamford Bridge hot-seat was Glenn Hoddle, appointed during the summer of 1993. After having had such a long lay-off, Cascarino was determined to make a good impression on his new boss.

"I liked some of his ideas, but his man-management left a lot to be desired. I'd got back into training early and I was fitter than I'd ever been. I was playing well, really flying, but Hoddle was determined to take all the credit."

The man who loomed largest over Chelsea during this time was, of course, the legendary Ken Bates. Much-maligned he may be, but Bates was proving himself a man of surprising vision, as Cascarino explains. "He showed us a model of how he wanted Stamford Bridge to look, with new stands and a hotel. This was in 1993, and we laughed then, but it's all come true. It was Ken who brought Ruud Gullit to the club, and all the big names came from there."

After a substitute appearance in the 1994 FA Cup final against Manchester United ("I came on when we were three down and the only difference I made was that we lost four-nil") Cascarino went off to the World Cup finals in the USA in the strange position of taking part in the biggest competition in football whilst at the same time facing unemployment on his return home after being given a free transfer by Hoddle. He had played in 40 league games for Chelsea, scoring eight goals. "I was in the team hotel getting faxes from teams like Reading and Notts County. John Sheridan, who was in the squad with me, said I should sign for Blackpool because they had a good Big Dipper at the funfair. Then Dennis Roach, my agent, told me that Olympique Marseilles were interested. I was 31 and on a free; they'd won the European Cup the year before. I told the rest of the Ireland squad and they were pissing themselves laughing."

But however unlikely it may have been, the interest from Marseilles was deadly serious. After being found guilty of match-fixing, they had been relegated from the top division of the French league, and, in serious financial straits, could only sign free transfers. "They were looking for an international striker who wouldn't cost them anything but, unsurprisingly, there weren't many of us around," says the man who was destined to be their biggest name.

Faced with a choice of the lower divisions in either England or France, Cascarino opted for life on the Mediterranean. His story could have ended there, but for one of the greatest transformations, both in personal and professional life, that has ever befallen an English player who moved overseas.

Cascarino, playing for a club that had grown used to success, began his Marseilles career with six goals in his first six games. Supporters who had previously idolised the likes of Chris Waddle and Jean-Pierre Papin, took this archetypal English centre-forward to their hearts.

"I knew that this was a big time for me. I got to peak fitness, lost half a stone, and I'd never felt so confident. We played Juventus in a friendly and Jurgen Kohler, the German international I'd faced in that summer's World Cup tournament, said that I'd run him ragged. He reckoned after the match that I was a different player. Juventus were looking to sign me, but I was 32 by then, and they lost interest when they realised my age."

Playing for Marseilles gave Cascarino first-hand knowledge of the club's infamous president, Bernard Tapie, a man who had brought fame to Marseilles, but whose dealings had also lead to their downfall. "He was mad, the biggest gangster I ever came across in football. If we lost he'd charge into the dressing room, grab players by the balls, insult them, rant away. He was a massive, bullying figure. Doug Ellis wasn't in the same league. As for Ken Bates, I'd rank him midway between the two of them."

Cascarino also blames Tapie for the dubious drugs with which he was injected during his time with Marseilles. "The club doctor regularly injected me, and the other players, with what he called an 'adrenaline-boosting' substance. I still don't know what it was, and I doubt if it was legal."

In just over two years at Marseilles, Tony found his life transformed. For the first time since his Millwall days he was scoring regularly, and found life in the Mediterranean port, whose football supporters are reckoned to be the most fanatical in France, suiting him perfectly. In particular, the hardcore ultras of Marseilles made a cult hero of the battling Cascarino. "Everyone seemed to like me. It was like living in a goldfish bowl seven days a week. If the team had lost or I played badly, though, I couldn't leave the house. We won Ligue 2, but were unable to get back into the top division because of the penalties imposed on us, then won the league again, and this time we got promotion. The coach, Gerard Gili, thought I wouldn't be able to score goals in Ligue 1, so I was given a free transfer at the beginning of the 1997-98 season."

Cascarino's phenomenal record of 61 goals in 84 games for Marseilles would have been a good enough end to anyone's career, but instead, it opened the way for another French move, albeit one that saw a brief return to Ligue 2. "I moved to Nancy, and in one of my first games I got a hat-trick at Le Havre. Then, on the way back home we found out that Marseilles had been beaten by Lille. Gili got sacked afterwards."

Cascarino's time with Nancy proved the most Indian of summers. His new club won Ligue 2, and the now-veteran striker, who had been written off years previously, found goals almost as easy to score in the top flight. "I'm so proud of what I did there," he says, understandably. "After we got promoted, I was awarded the

Medaille d'Or, the Gold Medal of Honour that is the highest award the city can bestow on its citizens. The only footballer to win the award before had been Michel Platini. Then, I scored 28 goals in two seasons in Ligue 1."

Unfortunately, Nancy were relegated at the end of the 1999-2000 season ("We went down with 42 points from 34 games. Bradford City survived in the Premiership with 35 points from 38 games") and Cascarino was, reluctantly, a luxury they could no longer afford. He moved to Red Star, a Parisienne team playing in the third, National level, of the French league, in front of crowds that regularly dropped to three figures, but his heart was no longer in the game. "I was so dejected when Nancy went down that I didn't want to play any more. I didn't train, I wasn't fit. I should have quit then but Red Star asked me to join them, so I signed up for a season. The set-up there was a joke, there was no proper training; everything was just amateurish. I made a couple of substitute appearances but I really didn't want to be there so I left after a month and retired from the game."

There are many careers open to former professional footballers. Tony Cascarino, naturally, found an opening in one of the more unusual ones. Divorced and living with the French mother of his young daughter, Cascarino was in no great hurry to return to England. "I became a professional poker player. Because I'd spent so long in France I was eligible for their welfare system, which provides earnings-related payments for anyone who's unemployed, on a sliding scale for up to three years. I was on the maximum, so at first I was getting three thousand pounds a month. I'd get up at midday, have lunch with my girlfriend and take our daughter to school, then, from six in the afternoon until 6 am I'd play poker in the Wagran casino on the Champs Elysses. I lost in the first year and won it all back in the second."

By now, Cascarino had become known as more than just another ex-footballer. "I'd spoken to Andy Townsend, who thought that I had a decent story to tell. He put me in touch with Paul Kimmage, who had written Andy's book about the 1994 World Cup, amongst others. Paul wasn't particularly interested at first, but later listened to me and said that he'd help me with my story. I'd read many books written by footballers, and I wanted to do something different. I wanted to be as honest about my life as I could. Paul came over to Nancy and we spent five hours a day for three days going through what would be in the book. Then three weeks later he said that the idea was a goer and it took him a year to do it properly."

The book, '*Full Time – The Secret Life of Tony Cascarino*,' caused a revelation when it was published in November 2000. Whilst in a wider context it will never be regarded as a great work of literature, the book was one of the most original and revealing football biographies ever written. Cascarino showed himself to be deeply insecure, lacking in confidence and very much an ordinary man, subject to the same indecisions and frailties as any of us. For those who regard sportsmen, and particularly footballers, as infallible gods, *Full Time* came as an eye-opener. "Everyone could relate to it. Before I wrote the book, no-one had ever thought that a footballer could be so driven with doubts that he'd be thinking during the game 'Don't pass to me'. People think that footballers live a fantasy life where nothing goes wrong, but the same sort of things that affect them affect us as well.

"The book did much the same thing for my state of mind that Tony Adams' confession that he was an alcoholic did for him. It allowed others to come forward and admit that they suffer from the same problem. Sonia O'Sullivan, for example. She's won world titles, set world records, but she now admits that if someone went past her in a race, she couldn't handle the pressure. I knew all about that; I'd been so short of confidence at Celtic that I'd asked to be put in the reserves."

The other sensation in *Full Time* was the announcement that Cascarino had not been eligible to play for the Republic of Ireland when first selected, as the grandmother who enabled him to qualify had been Irish by naturalisation, rather than by birth. "That was the hook I thought would attract much of the initial attention, so I was prepared for it. In the end it became irrelevant in the context of the rest of the book, but it helped bring out the element of black humour that runs throughout. Anyway, I got an Irish passport eventually."

Writing the book did more than exorcise the demons Cascarino had grappled with during his time on the pitch, it also provided the basis of what has up until now been a lucrative media career. "We didn't make much out of the book, but the spin-offs were good. Paul went to work at the *Sunday Times* and I got a column on their supplement, *The Game*. I also write for the *Racing Post*, and co-hosted Talksport's drive time programme with Patrick Kinghorn until February 2005. There was a bit of a clash of personalities there, so I left."

Cascarino's arrival in the ranks of the nation's sporting media has, of course, not been welcomed in all quarters. The sports editor of the *Mirror*, Oliver Holt, made a particularly snide attack when he described Cascarino as needing "a proper journalist to hold his hand." The reason for Holt's ire was that Cascarino had criticised Stan Collymore's autobiography 'Tackling My Demons'– a title Tony could have used himself, and which was ghost-written by the 'proper journalist' Oliver Holt. As Cascarino says, "I never deny that my columns are ghost-written, and for his part Holt has ghosted plenty of stories. It was all because I attacked Collymore's book, and after what he went on to do, I think I've been proved right. Boasting that he laughed when someone suffered a heart attack, how could Collymore do that?"

Tony Cascarino is certainly an honest man. In what can often be a nasty business, his honesty shines through. Even so, I wasn't prepared for the next bombshell. Asking him about his football career, he replied, "I wasn't much cop, really. I'm not gifted but in the right circumstances I can be effective. I'm six foot three and I can put myself about, but if I wasn't that size, I'd never have got anywhere."

It takes a few seconds for such a statement to sink in. Whatever you may think about Cascarino's ability, this is a player who reached heights comparatively few footballers could even dream about. He made 88 appearances for the Republic of Ireland at a time when they were one of the top national sides in the world, appearing in two World Cup finals tournaments. He had an eighteen-year professional career, featured in three big-money transfers and was still scoring goals in one of Europe's most competitive leagues at the age of 37. Tony Cascarino has every right to feel proud of his footballing achievements, yet he dismisses himself so lightly.

Now back living in Chislehurst, Kent, with his wife and having a son and daughter, Cascarino is enjoying life. He's a former international footballer, a 'motivational speaker,' professional poker player and now a media star. But ask him his greatest achievement and the answer might, if you've not read this chapter closely, surprise you.

"I turned my career round. There I was, aged 31 and just slung out by Chelsea. The rest of my career was mapped out from then on; Reading, Notts County, Blackpool, non-league within three years, then oblivion. But instead of that I turned it all round, I moved over to France and had another six great seasons in the game. My success wasn't about winning 88 caps or scoring so many goals. It's about how I was able to stop my own personal slide."

Graham Fenton

If the road to hell is paved with good intentions, then the road to footballing stardom is equally slabbed with promising youngsters who never made the big time. Villa Park crowds have witnessed many a young player explode on to the scene rich in promise, only to burn out before fulfiling their potential. Some failed to make the grade due to injury, or because they lacked the right attitude to make the transition from promising junior to fully-fledged star. Others were never as good as the rave initial reviews from the terraces held them to be. And the reason why some didn't become stars remains swathed in mystery long after they left Villa Park for the last time.

Graham Fenton, at first glance, belongs to the latter category. Anyone who witnessed the way he commanded the greatest stage in English football while still a teenager with a handful of Premier League appearances to his name would have thought a domestic cup final the first of many big occasions in which the combative midfielder-cum-striker would shine. That he was out of professional football within ten years shows football can not only be a rewarding game for a young player, it can also be a cruel one.

Born in the north-east town of Wallsend, in 1974, Fenton joined Villa as a YTS trainee at the age of 16. His first shot at the big time came when on loan to Albion during the 1993-94 season, where he made a big, although not entirely instant, impression, scoring four goals in seven games. "It was a big step up. I'd been playing for Villa reserves and suddenly I was performing in front of crowds of 15,000. It took me a couple of weeks to get adjusted. I didn't score for three games but I got three in my last three matches. Then it was back to Villa."

At that time the club were inundated with quality strikers. Dalian Atkinson and Dean Saunders were first choice pairing of manager

Ron Atkinson, with the likes of Dwight Yorke and future German international Stefan Beinlich in reserve. There seemed little chance of Fenton breaking into the side, but Big Ron was to think differently as the 1994 League Cup final against Manchester United came up. Fenton well remembers the approach to the club's date at Wembley. "I'd played a couple of first team games, but in the run-up to the final Ron said that nobody's place was safe. I went down to Bisham Abbey with the rest of the party a couple of days beforehand, and even though I was training with the first team I never thought I'd be playing. Then the eleven was announced and I was in. It was only my third or fourth game."

Fenton was, indeed, the surprise package of a Villa side that Atkinson picked with the aim of countering United's midfield strength. The 3-1 scoreline was an accurate reflection of ninety minutes in which that season's double-winners elect were comprehensively outplayed, much of the credit going to the youngest and most inexperienced player on the pitch, who completely outshone such established opponents as Eric Cantona and Paul Ince.

Fenton looked set for a career in the big time but, unfortunately, his subsequent Villa career was to prove as short-lived as Atkinson's. Winning the club's first trophy for twelve years proved no insurance for the manager against the wrath of Doug Ellis once results slumped at the start of the following season, and, with Villa fighting relegation, Atkinson found himself out of a job in November 1994.

New broom Brian Little was determined to shape the team in his own image, and Fenton was one of those deemed surplus to requirements, after having scored three goals in 18 starts, with an additional 21 appearances as a substitute. He says of the time, "I was naturally sorry to see Ron go; he had given me my opportunity. Brian came in, and he treated me well. He was a nice guy, he offered me a new contract but I felt that I deserved better terms than Villa were willing to pay me. There were players in the same position as me earning ten times the amount that I'd been offered. I was in the first-team squad and I wanted first-team wages. I didn't really want to go, but I got the feeling that I wasn't part of Brian's plans."

Express & Star journalist Martin Swain was as well-placed as anyone to comment on Fenton's time at Villa Park, and on his subsequent development. "Graham will always be remembered for that day at Wembley, when he did a fantastic job. He looked as though he could be the real thing – he had pace, drive, the lot, but he just never kicked on. Maybe the problem was that he never found his proper position, but whatever he did during the rest of his career, it was worth it just for that one afternoon."

And so, in November 1995, still barely out of his teens, Fenton made what at the time looked to be an attractive £1.5 million move to Blackburn Rovers, reigning Premiership holders – thanks to the help of multi-millionaire benefactor Jack Walker – and seemingly well-placed for a lucrative run in the Champions League. For a young player whose career had got off to such a good start it seemed an ideal situation, and Fenton recalls the appeal of the move. "Ewood Park seemed a great place to go. Expectations were sky-high, but in hindsight there was always a danger that Rovers would fall away after winning the title, and that's what happened. Two days after I joined, David Batty and Graeme Le Saux had their fight on the pitch in a Champions League game against Moscow Spartak, and that set the tone for the season. There wasn't a deep-rooted thing in the dressing room, no great split, it was just those two didn't get on. All the players respected Ray Harford, who was the manager at the time, and Kenny Dalglish, who had moved up to Director of Football. We hardly saw anything of Kenny from day to day, but he'd often turn up for training when we were playing five a side, and he'd be the best player on the pitch. I learnt a lot from him."

However much he may have gained from training alongside one of the great strikers of all time, Fenton found it difficult to get into the Blackburn first team, his way being blocked by another pair who have always known how to put the ball in the back of the net. "Alan Shearer and Chris Sutton," he reflects ruefully. "It was hard to get into the side. Looking back, it wasn't too clever of me to join a club that had four or five recognised strikers. I'd gone from being a reserve at Villa to the same situation with Blackburn"

Fenton spent two seasons at Ewood Park, playing in 16 games, with another 21 substitute appearances, although he managed to score seven goals, including two in five minutes against his boyhood idols Newcastle as the Geordies title hopes slipped away in a 2-1 defeat during April 1996. Blackburn by then had long-since relinquished their crown and were beginning to slide from the higher echelons of the league table. Much of the reason was that Sky's riches had started to take effect throughout the top flight and a mere multi-millionaire was no longer sufficiently wealthy to bankroll a club who would never be well-supported, no matter how many trophies they won. "Maybe Jack had done all he wanted when they won the league and he didn't want to spend much more money. Whatever happened, the big signings stopped and Rovers couldn't stay up there at the top."

New manager Roy Hodgson came in to replace Ray Harford, and the arrival of Swedish international Martin Dahlin was the final signal to Fenton that his future was no longer in Lancashire. "I had a choice of going back to Albion, who were still in the first division, or to Leicester, who'd just won the League Cup, so they were playing in Europe. It didn't seem like much of a choice, but it turned into the worst mistake of my life."

Fenton moved to Filbert Street in August 1997, for a fee of £1.1 million, but soon realised that he should have taken his chances in the West, rather than the East, Midlands. Martin O'Neill may have earned a reputation as one of the best managers in the game through his work at Filbert Street and then with Celtic, but he certainly didn't impress Graham Fenton. "We didn't get on," says the player. "It was a clash of personalities. I like to be praised if I've done well, but I never got any of that at Leicester and it affected my game. Look at Ron Atkinson, for example. He used to send you out on to the pitch thinking you were the best player in the world, and you'd respond. O'Neill had me thinking that I couldn't play.

"He must be a good manager, his record speaks for itself, but he wasn't for me. There was also a problem in that with Villa and Blackburn I always received good service from the rest of the team. Without being detrimental to Leicester, they never gave me that support."

Fenton stayed at Filbert Street for two seasons, scoring three goals in 34 games, but missing out on another League Cup final appearance when the club lost to Spurs in 1999. "I'd scored in the earlier rounds, but never got picked for Wembley." He then moved to Walsall on loan in March 2000. Here, he came across another former Villa connection, in the shape of Saddlers' boss Ray Graydon, and played eight games, scoring one goal, as Walsall battled in vain to stay in the first division. Of his temporary boss, Fenton says, "Ray was an old-school manager, strict but always fair with us. You could talk to him. I enjoyed my time at Walsall, but I didn't stay on at the end of the season because they'd just been relegated and I thought I could still do a job in the first division."

Given a free transfer by Leicester, Fenton then moved to Stoke City at the beginning of the 2000-01 season, enjoying a brief spell at the Britannia Stadium before falling foul of footballing politics. "John Rudge got me there on the premise that, if I proved my fitness, they'd offer me a contract. I played for a month, did okay, and then they only offered me another month. I needed more security than that, so I wasn't best pleased. The final insult came when the Icelander who ran the club signed a Scandinavian forward, and it was obvious that they'd just used me as a stop-gap." Graham had played four games for Stoke, scoring once.

Unable to get fixed up with an English club, Fenton took advantage of the opportunities now opening in Scottish football, only to find the realities of life outside the Old Firm an eye-opener as he signed for St Mirren, newly-promoted to the Scottish Premier League, at the end of September 2000. "Saints offered me a two-year deal, which was fair enough, and the money was good. They'd just got promoted, and I didn't think it would be as hard to stay in the Premier as it was. We went to Ibrox; we thought we'd give it a go and play 4-3-3. We lost 7-1. Then, at Celtic, we were fired up and I maybe tried too hard."

Life in Scotland had its ups and downs for a young footballer. "We were living in the West End of Glasgow, a beautiful part of town. The Scots were great, they have an affinity with Geordies and I got on well with everyone. I did have one problem, though. A watch I owned worth a couple of thousand pounds was stolen from the dressing room. We all had a fair idea who took it, but there was no evidence to prosecute him. At the end of the season, St Mirren got relegated and the wage drop meant that it wasn't worth staying with them, so I took advantage of the get-out clause in my contract and headed home." His time in Scotland had seen Graham playing 26 games for St Mirren, during which he scored two goals.

The 2001-02 season began with Fenton training at third division Darlington, and here he impressed the management, who offered a contract. However, a more attractive proposition then came along. "Steve McMahon wanted me to sign for him at Blackpool, who were in division two. Everything was fine at first; we were playing nice football and I was getting on well with Steve. He treated some of the other players badly, though. You shouldn't treat experienced pros like that, making them train with the youth team. Eventually we had a falling out. It was at the start of my second season there; I'd had a couple of injuries and my fitness had dropped a bit, so I felt out of it." Fenton had played ten games for Blackpool, scoring five goals.

He remembers this as a time when his personal and professional lives were at a low ebb. "It was a bad time for me personally – my dad had just died, and I wanted to go back home. I'd been on loan to Darlington, and I'd done alright there, playing six games and scoring, so they offered me a contract. Unfortunately, it was the time when George Reynolds was chairman and the money they offered was just silly. I couldn't accept such a low figure, so I thought it was about time I stepped out of league football and got myself a proper job."

And with that decision, made after careful consideration and with no little regret, one of English football's most promising players of the nineties ended his professional career in late 2002, at the age of 28. Not for Graham Fenton the lucrative and glamorous entrance into the media that the big names can obtain once they hang up their boots. "I took a year out, looking after my young family, and now I'm waiting for the fire brigade to start recruiting so I can join them."

Fenton is now playing football with Blyth Spartans of the Unibond Northern League, in front of crowds a fraction the size of those that witnessed his triumphant arrival into the Premiership. While the opposition might not be up to the same standard, the challenge, though different, is still difficult. "It's hard to get used to the kind of surfaces we play on. I was a bit inconsistent in my first season, but I've settled down a bit now. I've dropped back into midfield and I find that much easier than when I was playing up front. "

Of course, being a big name by non-league standards means that Fenton can often be a marked man, in more ways than one. "I've been targeted by one or two defenders, and I've also been made a bit of a scapegoat, particularly when some of the crowd thought I was earning a lot more than I was. The players knew what the truth was, but for a long time the fans were a different matter."

Fenton spent part of the 2004-05 season making his first foray into management – as Blyth's caretaker-manager – before taking on the role as player-assistant manager when the permanent job was given to Harry Dunn. He now lives in North Shields with his wife. They have one child with, as he puts it, "another on the way."

Looking back on his career, Fenton obviously has one regret, and it provides the answer to those who might ask 'Whatever happened to Graham Fenton?'

"Joining Leicester. I lost all confidence; in all the time I was there, I'd go out on to the pitch and I never thought I would be involved in the game. Those three years cost me my career." Sometimes, a mystery that seems unfathomable to the outsider is no mystery at all.

Tony Hateley

On my way to meeting Tony Hateley, I got lost. It wasn't his fault; I misunderstood the directions he'd given and ended up a few miles from where I intended. The result was that when I arrived at the Hateley residence on the outskirts of Preston, Tony was already waiting outside. I got the impression that being late is not a thing Tony Hateley appreciates, which is only natural for a man whose footballing career was built around split-second timing.

Born in Derby in 1941, Hateley left school to become an apprentice woodcutting machinist, signing for Notts County on his seventeenth birthday. He says of those days, "I'd started a team called Normanton Sports with a few friends, and four of us were training twice a week at County. Tommy Lawton was their manager, with the old Villa player Frank Broome as his assistant. County were the bigger team in Nottingham in those days, and were regularly getting gates of over twenty thousand."

Hateley scored 82 goals in 150 games for Notts before moving to Villa in 1963 as a replacement for the inconsistent Derek Dougan at a cost of £25,000. The promise of the early part of Joe Mercer's reign was beginning to fade, and, as one of the few players at the club who had been signed for a large fee, Tony bore much of the supporters' criticism for the team's failings at the time. This was despite a fine goalscoring record, which saw him hit the back of the net regularly during his spell at Villa Park. Dave Collett, a regular on the Holte End at the time, says of the player, "For some reason he couldn't do anything right for some people. If he scored from thirty yards they'd want to know why he hadn't scored from forty. If he scored two they'd moan that he hadn't got a hat-trick."

Hateley himself remains, with some justification, unconcerned about this aspect of his Villa Park career. "It wasn't a problem for me. I was young and I'd done quite well at Notts. Maybe the trouble was that I never stopped living in Derby. I travelled in to Villa for training every day and afterwards I'd have a bath and then go straight home. I scored so many goals that all I ever heard at Villa Park was cheers, anyway."

So well did Hateley play for Villa that he was on the fringes of the England squad for the 1966 World Cup, until fate took a hand. "We were playing Spurs and I got a bad injury that kept me out for a few months. By the time I was fully fit the squad was sorted. Geoff Hurst had made his late run into Alf Ramsey's plans, and you can't really say that Alf made a mistake there."

With Villa in decline, it was obvious that Tony Hateley would not be with the club for much longer. A fee of £100,000 was agreed with Chelsea, and Hateley moved to Stamford Bridge in 1966, a few months before Villa were relegated to the second division at the beginning of what would prove to be an eight-year exile from the top flight. Tony's record of 86 goals in 148 games stands comparison with any in the Villa's history, and he obviously enjoyed his time in Aston. "I didn't want to leave Villa, but the board couldn't turn down that sort of fee," is his comment on the circumstances surrounding what was an inevitable departure.

But, even then, the transfer wasn't as straightforward as it seemed, as Hateley reveals. "I was originally going to Liverpool; then Peter Osgood broke his leg playing for Chelsea. Bill Shankly agreed that Chelsea could buy me, and then they'd sell me on to Liverpool when Osgood was fit, for the price they'd paid Villa. That was fine by me.

"I scored a few for Chelsea, and we got to the cup final that season, although Spurs beat us thanks to a couple of fluky goals. Then, when Osgood came back, I was off to Anfield. The trouble was, though, that this was the year when the top level of income tax was 19/6 in the pound, so although I was involved in two £100,000 transfers, I hardly saw a penny of the signing-on fees."

Chico Hamilton played for Chelsea on a couple of occasions with Hateley. He remembers "An old-fashioned centre-forward. Tony would dish it out and take it with the best." In all, Hateley played for Chelsea on 32 occasions, scoring nine goals.

Tony spent just over a season with Liverpool, and, although he scored a respectable 28 goals in 56 games, his period at Anfield was not as successful as it might have been, coming at a time when the team was in the process of being rebuilt. "Ian St John and Roger Hunt were both drawing to the end of their great careers, although Roger and I scored a load of goals in my first season. In the end Bill Shankly sold me shortly after the beginning of the 1968-69 season because he said I was injury-prone. I wasn't going to argue with him – there was never any point in arguing with Shanks.

"I ended up signing for Coventry for £80,000. Noel Cantwell had taken Jimmy Hill's place as manager, but they were still an ambitious club. I lasted there a year, then I was off to Birmingham." Hateley's spell at Coventry was a short one, comprising 20 appearances, during which time he scored five goals.

Unfortunately, his career at St Andrews lasted no longer, and was not one upon which he now looks back with any great fondness. "Stan Cullis signed me, then three weeks later he was sacked and Freddie Goodwin came in. We didn't get on; I used to ask him why I wasn't in the first team and he'd say, 'You'll play when I tell you you're playing'. Then he'd stick me in the reserves at centre-half."

During this period of exile away from first team football, Hateley became aware of a youngster by the name of Trevor Francis. "He used to clean my boots. You could hardly say he had a normal upbringing, what with being a first team regular when he was 16, but anyone could see that he had fabulous talent."

His second spell with a Birmingham club obviously not working out, Tony resorted to subterfuge to get the move that would otherwise have proved impossible in those days before players enjoyed freedom of contract. "I was told that Notts County were in for me, but I knew that Goodwin was reluctant to let me go. So I made an appointment to see my doctor, and before I went in to see him I rubbed my eyes, then gave a bit of a sob story about how I was having a terrible time, how I couldn't sleep and was having migraines. He agreed to sign me off sick for six months, so I just went and did a bit of training, and Jimmy Sirrell, who was County manager at the time, came in with an offer but said he'd reduce it by a thousand pounds for every day he had to wait. Goodwin knew he couldn't do anything with me, so he agreed and I was off to County for £32,000." Hateley had played 29 times for Birmingham, scoring six goals before his return to Meadow Lane in September 1970.

By now the situation at Meadow Lane was different from the one that Hateley had left some nine years earlier. "Gates were down to six or seven thousand, then the first match I was back they got some 25,000-odd." And it wasn't only at the turnstiles that the Hateley magic was seen. "We won the fourth division by Christmas that season. We must have had the tallest team ever – Don Masson was the captain, David Needham was just starting out, he went on to win the European Cup with Forest. I was one of the shortest players in the team. We battered everybody."

During his second spell at Meadow Lane, Hateley proved the exception to the rule of never going back. He scored 35 goals in 57 games, helping County to win the fourth division title and then narrowly miss out on promotion to the second the following season. Tony moved to Oldham during the summer of 1972, although his career with the Lancashire side was limited to just one full appearance with four more as a substitute, scoring a single goal, before injury put paid to one of the greatest goalscoring careers English football has ever seen. "I'd had a few problems with my knees, then while I was at Oldham I asked Jimmy McDowell, who was their physio, what the problem was. He told me that, basically, my knee was totally knackered and advised me to pack in playing. I had five operations all told – there was nothing left to operate on in the end. It was like butchery in those days. Nowadays it's all pinhole surgery, but when I was playing we'd spend a fortnight in hospital with a leg in traction."

Hateley spent the 1974-75 season playing for Bromsgrove Rovers, of the Southern League and then settled down to a job as a salesman for the Thwaite's brewery, in Lancashire. "I was involved on the free trade side. It was a great job, especially when I worked on Merseyside. I'd walk into a pub and, being an ex-Liverpool player, I could sell them anything. I was moved to the Preston area after a few years and stayed there until I left the brewery in 1996. I retired then, and I'm loving it."

'Retired' he may be, but inactive Tony Hateley most certainly is not. "I first met Norman Wisdom round about 1980, and we helped to organise the SPARKS charity, which helped disabled children. That evolved into the Celebrity Golf Tour, which to date has raised £3.5 million for various charities. We have plenty of sports stars and entertainers involved, although I'm not able to play as much as I'd like now. Every year we have around 40 events and raise anything up to £350,000. I'm also on the committee of the Liverpool Former Players' Association"

Hateley also draws much of his inspiration from his family: a son and daughter, plus eight grandchildren and two great-grandchildren. His son is, of course, former England international Mark. "We are the only father and son to have scored 200 league goals each," Tony says with understandable pride.

Indeed, a comment about Mark's ability to seemingly hang in the air, as he often showed during his successful period with Rangers, was enough excuse for Tony to spring to his feet and, in the living room of his Preston home, provide me with a master-class in the art of jumping for a cross. "I taught him how to do it, " he commented. "You jump a split-second before the defender, then put your elbow on his shoulder and he pushes you up higher." And with those sage words of advice imbedded into my head I left the Hateley household a slightly wiser man, even if it was twenty years too late to improve my footballing prospects.

Keith Leonard

There was a time during the late seventies when it appeared that the Villa team coach must have run over a black cat on the way to a game, such was the run of serious injuries that affected the playing squad and hampered Ron Saunders' attempts to rebuild following the League Cup triumph of 1977. Brian Little, Mike Pejic, Alex Cropley and, most tragic of all, John Robson, were just some of the names who found their careers either disrupted or coming to a premature end during this time. It was small wonder that amongst this collection of great names, Keith Leonard's brief but promising period at Villa Park often gets overlooked.

Leonard was born in Solihull, in 1950, and made a comparatively late start into professional football. "I was a draughtsman when I left school. I was playing for Kidderminster Harriers reserves, then I went to Darlaston, in the West Midlands League, then moved to Highgate in the Midland Combination. Walsall came in for me, but Villa were interested and I signed in April 1972, after a week's trial."

Easing his way on to the fringes of the first team under Vic Crowe, Keith made four appearances for the side in the 1973-74 season, until a broken leg suffered in a car accident put him out of the game for eighteen months. By the time he was back in first team contention Ron Saunders was Villa manager and, with the aid of what was for Keith a fortuitous injury to Sammy Morgan, the local-born centre-forward became established in the Villa front-line in time to play a major part in the successful promotion push and League Cup final of 1945-75.

A long career in the first division looked on the cards, but during his fourth match in the top flight, at home to Arsenal, Keith suffered the injury that was to finish his playing career after just 45 games, in which he had scored 17 goals. He says of the incident, "I was hurt in a collision with Jimmy Rimmer, who was the Arsenal 'keeper. It didn't seem much when it happened, but the knee swelled up at half-time and again after the match, then complications set in. Things are different now, with the new advances in surgery there'd be a 99% chance of making a full recovery, but back then it was no better than 50-50 and I was one of the unlucky ones. You'd be in hospital for a fortnight, but now it's not even an overnight stay – just keyhole surgery and often the cartilage doesn't even have to be removed."

Leonard spent more than a year struggling to return to full fitness, but, with arthritis damaging the knee, he was finally forced to quit football and, at the age of 28, face an uncertain future. "Luckily, Ron Saunders helped me out. He offered to let me do some coaching, just learning the ropes, and when Frank Upton, who was the youth team coach, left to go to Chelsea, Ron asked me to be his replacement."

It's always hard for a former player to watch from the sidelines, but it must be made even more difficult to be an onlooker as former team-mates go on to conquer Europe. Leonard remains philosophical about the fact that the Villa's early eighties triumphs could so easily have featured him. "I had my time, and they had theirs. All the success came three or four years after I retired, and who knows what might have happened to me in the meantime? It was a bit hard being in charge of them at first, though. There was one occasion when we were in pre-season training and all the lads had to run up the hills at Bodymoor Heath. That was always one of the things I hated most when I was a player, so when I was telling the lads to start running there was a bit of back-chat"

Leonard was instrumental in shaping the Villa youth policy of the late seventies, one which provided the backbone of the first-team's success during the years that followed. However, even the best youth set-up will inevitably have the ones that got away.

"Brian McClair always had talent, but in the end we let him go because we had so many players who were all much of a muchness. There wasn't anything about Brian that really stood out, so we released him. He went back home, signed for Motherwell, and he never looked back. Celtic, Manchester United, Scotland: he had a great career."

Villa's success in the early eighties naturally provided the club with a great boost, but for promising youngsters the success was double–edged. "There were a lot of promising young players at the club, but they just couldn't get into the side because the first team were so good. Brendan Ormsby, for example. England youth team captain, a great prospect, but he couldn't shift Ken McNaught and Allan Evans from the first team, and when either of them were injured, Ron would move Gary Williams into the centre of the defence and shuffle things round to keep the continuity going."

As a former youth coach, Leonard is ideally placed to comment on the most important aspects of a club's youth set-up. "If you get two or three players who make the grade at the first team's level over a three-year cycle, you've done well. It doesn't matter whether you're in the Premier League or the bottom division, if you can get them into your first team you've done a good job." Of course, for the rest it can be an unforgiving business. "The worst job in football is telling an 18 year old that they aren't going to make it. They've had that dream maybe all their life, then in a minute it's over and you're the one who has to tell them. The first time I had to tell an apprentice that we were letting him go was hardest thing I've ever had to do in my life – and it never got any easier."

However, at a club such as Villa, where standards are so high that only the very best are offered professional contracts, there is often a second chance for those who fall by the wayside. "The best example of this was Brian McClair, again. Leaving Villa was the making of him. Motherwell converted him from a striker into a midfielder and made him realise that he was good enough."

Of course, whatever ups and downs Villa Park has witnessed over the years, little can top the momentous few months at the beginning of 1982 when, first, Ron Saunders walked out on his job as manager of the league champions, and then the club celebrated winning the European Cup. By the time of the latter occurrence, Keith Leonard was no longer in the Villa's employ as a direct result of the former bombshell, which had occurred some three months earlier.

However, anyone who might think that one of Saunders' closest aides may be able to shed some light on the mystery of why he quit Villa Park will be disappointed. "I don't know why Ron left Villa, although I suspect that he just didn't get on with the Bendalls. It was his team that won the European Cup. Everyone knows that. But the players also knew that fresh blood was needed and the money wasn't there. Anyway, he moved to Blues, asked me to join him and I became his first-team coach."

It's fair to say that the Saunders era is not remembered with great fondness at St Andrews, although there are Villa supporters who claim, only half-jokingly, that it was all a ploy on behalf of the manager to bring about the ruination of Villa's local rivals after he had set their own team up for unparalleled success. Leonard, though, defends his former boss. "When Ron arrived at St Andrews there were a lot of players who saw Blues as a meal ticket. Players such as Archie Gemmill and Frank Worthington – they'd been good in their day, but their day was gone, yet they were still on top wages. The club had spent the money they'd received for Trevor Francis on transfer fees, but they still had to pay the wages and there wasn't enough coming in."

And of course, Leonard was another ex-Villa man able to see at first hand the problems that Blues' players were causing off the field. "It was an on-going saga. Mark Dennis was typical – good enough to be an England youth international, but off the field he could be out of control. We had some decent players coming through the ranks – Julian Dicks and David Seaman, who signed from Peterborough. After David's first training session with us, Ron turned to me and said 'He'll play for England.' But when you have a whole bunch of players causing problems, you can't really discipline them all. You can't suspend them all together."

Saunders left St Andrews in January 1986, with Blues bound for a quick return to the second division. Gates were down, crowd problems endemic and the club had just endured the embarrassment of a 2-1 defeat at home to non-league Altrincham in the FA Cup third round. Unsurprisingly, this is not a period Leonard looks back upon with any great fondness. "Things were going wrong all over the place. We were going to grounds knowing that we were just there to make the numbers up and even if the lads gave their all, which they did week after week, it still wouldn't be enough. Ken Wheldon was chairman and it was a nightmare time. He was obsessed with cutting costs – there was a story that he went round the offices taking out light bulbs if he thought they weren't being used."

Leonard also left when Saunders departed, the two men teaming up once more when the manager joined Albion. Again, this was not a happy time for the pair. "Things were much the same at the Hawthorns as they had been at Blues. There were some good players around, or at least they'd been good players once, the likes of Steve McKenzie and Garth Crooks. They were decent footballers but they weren't going to do a club like Albion, who were on the slide and looking to cut costs, any favours. Garth Crooks, for example, was commuting from London into training ever day, so he must have been on big money, but he never showed any commitment to moving up to the area.

"Ron was brought in to do a job, to cut the wage bill, and the board were happy for him to take the stick from the supporters. It was the same situation that we'd had at Blues. The board used Ron as a way of deflecting the criticism from them because the club was in trouble. That was his problem after he left Villa, he took on clubs where he had nothing to work with."

Saunders finally left the Hawthorns, and football, in 1987, settling for a quiet life in retirement. He has rarely been heard of since. Leonard was not long in following his former boss out of the game, although he still needed to find employment. "I thought it was about time I got a proper job. I was coming up to 37, which would have been about the time I'd have packed in playing anyway, so I hadn't missed much. I took over a sub-post office in Chadwick, just outside Solihull, and we worked at that for eight years. Then things started getting a bit tighter. The Post Office were closing a lot of branches, so we sold the shop and I worked for the Post Office as a relief manager for a couple of years before I fancied another change. I went to work at Land Rover, which was a big change from running a shop in a small village. The first day I was there, on the assembly line, I thought 'I'll never manage this' but I've been there for 13 years."

Stepping into the real world was, naturally, a culture shock for a man who had enjoyed such a long career in football. "I'd always worked outside, playing and training. It was strange to be stuck inside all day, but I've got used to it now. I suppose that when I was in football I didn't ever think about the day when I'd have to work outside the game. It's a bit like getting a pension; you think you can just keep putting it off. I could have done a college day release course when I was a player, but I didn't bother."

Having to start afresh, competing in a crowded job market with rivals who may have twenty years greater experience in the commercial world, is a common problem for those who leave football. Leonard is honest enough to say that what seemed at the time the easy option might not, in the long-term, have been for the best. "Maybe it would have been better if I hadn't gone into coaching when I retired, if I'd had a clean break from the game so that I was still only about 27 when I had to look for another career. But when a Harley Street specialist tells you that your career is over, and you've only go six months left on your contract, you don't really think long-term. Ron offered me a job and I was grateful."

Leonard still lives close to the area in which he grew up and, married with three sons, there remains a professional sportsman bearing the Leonard name. "My son, James, is a polo player. He got into horse riding when he was younger and he plays for the Midas club, based at the Guards Polo Club in London. He's in New Zealand at the moment."

And as a salutary lesson of what lies ahead for all footballers, Keith Leonard still suffers as a result of that seemingly-innocuous challenge which changed his life almost thirty years ago. "I still have trouble with my knee. I was in hospital just before Christmas 2004 to have it washed out, and the joint still needs relining, although I keep putting it off because the operation only has a ten-year lifespan. It's a lucky footballer who goes through his career without a serious injury." Like too many of his contemporaries, Keith Leonard, sadly, was not one of the lucky ones.

Andy Lochhead

The trouble with growing up is that you realise your heroes aren't what you'd always imagined them to be. Chico Hamilton doesn't live share a leather-furnished penthouse with a dozen Page Three models. Brian Little can't walk on water – well, not quite. Debbie Harry never did understand that what she really wanted out of life was a younger man from the English Midlands. And Andy Lochhead doesn't breakfast on raw goalkeepers and dine on lightly boiled centre-halves, washed down with the blood of dismembered referees.

Born in Milingavie, near Glasgow, in 1941, Lochhead began his working life at the John Brown shipyards of Clydebank, as an apprentice sheet metal worker. At the same time, he spent what was euphemistically called his leisure hours playing in the sometimes-open warfare that is the Scottish junior set-up, itself the launch-pad for many a glittering football career.

"I worked in the shipyards for two years. I was playing for Drumchapel Amateurs, which was the team another worker on the docks played for a few years later, a lad named Alex Ferguson. Then I moved to Renfrew Juniors. The set-up at that level was a good introduction to football – you had to learn quickly if you were going to survive in it. Jimmy Stein, who was Burnley's scout up in Scotland at the time, recommended me to the club and I was asked if I wanted to sign professional, which I did, in 1958. I was on £8 a week, and it was a twelve-month contract, which was all we ever got back then."

"Burnley had a good team at the time, and they also had Bob Lord as chairman." The legendary supremo of Turf Moor enjoyed a reputation that lives on, even years after his death. As Andy remembers, "If he said it was Sunday, it was Sunday. But he did well for the club, you can't argue with that."

The Lochhead arrival in Lancashire coincided with a glorious period in Burnley's history, during which they won the league title in 1960, reached the FA Cup final two years later and made several appearances in European competition. Andy, however, plays down his role in the club's glory years. "I didn't have much of a run during my early days. The club felt that new players had to prove their worth, so although I made my debut in 1960, it was a couple of years before I was a regular in the side."

Lochhead established himself as a firm favourite with the Burnley crowd. Dave Thomas, writer of the book '*It's Burnley Not Barcelona*', says of Lochhead's time at Turf Moor, "Just the appearance of his name on a team sheet made many an opposing goalkeeper hapless. When challenging for any high ball, he reduced many a centre-half to dithering gibberishness."

In total, Andy played 226 times for Burnley, his 101 goals making him the last Clarets' player to score over a hundred times for the Lancashire club. Andy gained a solitary cap for the Scottish under-23 side when he lined up alongside his future team-mate Charlie Aitken against their Welsh counterparts. Of his brief international recognition he says, "They reckoned I was in line for a full call-up, but Scotland had a great set of forwards then and I never got a look-in." Andy then moved to Leicester City for a fee of £80,000 in 1968.

Lochhead enjoyed mixed fortunes at Leicester, appearing in their FA Cup final defeat at the hands of Manchester City in 1969, the same season as the Filbert Street club had been relegated from the first division. He made 44 league appearances, scoring 12 goals, before the newly-appointed Villa manager, Vic Crowe, paid £35,000 to bring Lochhead to Villa Park in an attempt to keep Villa out of the third division in 1970. Sadly, despite an upturn in the team's form, Andy was unable to prevent Villa's slide as he suffered his second consecutive relegation. And as Villa began the following season finding out that an immediate return would prove harder than anticipated, supporters found that their misfiring centre-forward made an easy scapegoat. "I had a lean spell, I'll admit that," is his honest assessment of those times. "And I took a bit of stick from the crowd."

However, as Villa's two-year spell in the third division came to prove a golden period in the memories of all supporters present during that bittersweet time, so Andy Lochhead won them over with a series of performances that would show the veteran Scotsman to be a worthy successor, in effort at least, to the great centre-forwards who had worn the claret and blue number nine shirt before him. Four matches stick out in the memory of everyone who witnessed them, and Lochhead naturally has vivid recollections of them all. "The Manchester United semi-final. What a great night that was. The supporters were tremendous in the second leg, they got us back into the game after we'd gone a goal down. Just before half-time Brian Godfrey hit a long ball. I went for it with Ian Ure, the United centre-half, and it ended up in the top corner. The Holte End was roaring us on and Pat McMahon got the winner late on."

Villa's performance in the subsequent final against Spurs saw them give one of the top sides in the country an almighty scare before going down to two late Martin Chivers goals. Andy's shot, which was cleared off the line by Steve Perryman, of which he now says, "I thought I'd been pulled up for a foul so I just stroked the ball towards the net and Steve could clear it away. The ref hadn't given the foul," was the deciding factor in a pulsating game.

However, the memorable cup run had also left too much to do in the promotion race. The club had to settle for fourth spot and a successful 1971-72 season, winning the third division title with a record 70 points and with two more memorable occasions along the way. A then-record third division gate of 48,110 saw Andy grab the winner in a game with fellow-promotion hopefuls Bournemouth. Villa had gone a goal down to a Ted McDougall header with Geoff Vowden equalising before Andy popped up in the dying stages of the game. "A free-kick came over. I went up for it. The ball flew up and dropped in just the right place for me to volley into the back of the net. That was another one when the crowd helped us."

And finally, the night when more than 53,000 packed into Villa Park to watch the friendly with Santos. "My vivid memory of that game was the argument over who should have Pele's shirt. Ron Wylie organised a draw and Pat McMahon ended up with it."

Chico Hamilton certainly enjoyed playing with Lochhead, "Andy was wonderful. We'd hit the corners over and he'd be flicking them on or else getting a header on target and usually scoring. There wasn't a defender who could get near him." Ray Graydon, the provider of many of Lochhead's goals in the title-winning season, described him as "A fine target man; always up there in the middle of it."

Andy finished the season with 25 goals, and was a worthy winner of the Midlands Player of the Year trophy, as well as the Terrace Trophy as Villa supporters' Player of the Season. 1972-73 saw him struggle to reproduce this form at a higher level, and in the summer of 1973, Lochhead was sold to third division side Oldham Athletic for £30,000. In total, he played 149 league games for Villa, scoring 44 goals. His value to the club, though, had been far greater than mere statistics can convey. Andy became a talismanic figure, a symbol of how the combined effort of players, supporters and everyone else connected with the club could, by sheer weight of effort, turn round decades of decline and provide a base for the success that was to come over the next ten years. He says of the end to his Villa career, "I didn't really want to go. I was enjoying playing with Brian Little; he had ability that was second to none, and I was doing fine with Alun Evans as well. But Doug Ellis said to me, 'You're going,' and that was that."

Lochhead began his Oldham career as a player, eventually becoming player-coach prior to hanging up his boots. "Bobby Collins left to manage Huddersfield, so there was a vacancy as a coach, and the Oldham manager of the time, Jimmy Frizzell, gave me the job. I knew I was coming to the end of my playing career, so it was a useful start in coaching." Although he never returned to Villa Park as a player, there was room for one last farewell which proved that Villa supporters will always remember with fondness a former hero who gave his all in the service of the club.

As the promotion bandwagon inspired by Ron Saunders rolled on, Oldham were the visitors to Villa Park on 5th April 1975, for a second division match. The result was a routine 3-0 home win. The afternoon, however, was made the more memorable for the reception accorded to the visiting side's coach. From the moment that Lochhead stepped on to the running track, in full view of those who had once adored him as a player, the crowd, to a man, rose to acclaim one of their heroes. Lochhead himself remembers the occasion perfectly, even though it was more than thirty years ago: "Tremendous. Very moving. Terrific. They applauded me all the way along the touch-line." And he deserved no less.

Andy played for Oldham for two seasons, making 45 appearances and scoring 10 goals. There was also time for a brief spell in the North American Soccer League, which at the time was providing a welcome and lucrative summer refuge for off-duty English footballers. "I had the chance to pay for Denver Dynamos. Ken Bracewell was their coach. He was from Nelson in Lancashire, and he took a few players from that area. There were three of us from Oldham, a couple of lads from Bury, Stockport, teams like that. We were never up to the standard of New York Cosmos, who had Pele and Franz Beckenbauer playing for them, or Tampa Bay with George Best, but it was an enjoyable summer. I took my wife and children over; we had a villa at the foot of the Rockies, complete with a swimming pool and a big American car provided. We'd fly to most of the away games and I visited New York, Los Angeles, all those places I'd dreamed of seeing."

Denver is known for its altitude; in fact, the ground where the Dynamos played was called the Mile High Stadium. Andy soon found out that although Boundary Park has a reputation as one of the most wind-swept grounds in England, it came nowhere near to preparing him for the rigours of 'soccer' Colorado-style. "They had oxygen tanks and masks on the touchline, all round the pitch. None of us could work out what they were for until the first match when we realised that if you were going to run around that high up you'd need oxygen soon enough. It didn't bother me so much, though. By that stage of my career I was just hanging around the opposition penalty area and scoring a few goals. In fact, I got a trophy for the first goal ever scored in the stadium. Until then it had been used for American football and baseball. It was mainly grass, but one end where the baseball took place was ash, and I got the first goal there."

The standard of football might not have been all it could have during the short-lived days of the NASL, but Lochhead saw one aspect in which the Americans had developed the game ahead of their European counterparts, and it was to have an effect on his life many years later.

"The PR campaign they put on for us was tremendous. There was all the razzmatazz you came to expect from the Americans, and they got us out into the schools, coaching the children because they thought the game would take off over there. The trouble, though, was that the children weren't used to a non-stop game. They played stop-start games such as American football and baseball, so they found it difficult. Ironically, it was the girls who took to our football a lot better than the boys. I wasn't surprised when the women's leagues took off as well as they did in the States, because girls had a lot more ability than the boys."

Back home, Andy settled down to life at Oldham, who continued to jog along in the old second division, never looking in danger of relegation, but unable to make much headway in competition with the Manchester giants. Andy had, by now, also added a second string to his bow in the most traditional of careers to which ex-footballers find themselves drawn. "Our local pub was the Bay Horse at Worstthorne. It had been thriving in the sixties, and although trade had declined, the brewery spent £40,000 on renovations when I applied to be the licensee. When we started out my wife, Carol, was in sole charge but as it took off it became more of an eating place and we had live music, so it was too much for her to run on her own."

Luckily for the pub trade, if not necessarily for Andy's footballing career, fate was to take a hand. "It was 1979. I'd enjoyed my time at Oldham; we'd never been very successful but we'd done alright. Then one day I was called into the chairman's office and informed that I was being 'relieved of my duties,' as the phrase goes. They wanted a change-round, and that was it. I was now helping to run a pub full-time. We stayed at the Bay Horse for ten years in all, then, in 1990, we took over running the Hightenmount Bowls Club, back in Burnley. We were there for six years."

Lochhead had settled comfortably into the life of an ex-professional footballer, yet the game, and the contacts he'd made therein, wouldn't leave him alone. "When I was at Oldham, they were so short of money that the groundsman, Jimmy Wibberley, had to double as the coach driver. He also started his own plumbing business, which did so well that he ended up with 250 employees and the contract to install meters for North West Water. I was looking for a change, so he offered me a job liaising with customers. I'd go along, tell them that they had to have a meter installed, sometimes whether they liked it or not, and make sure that the jobs were done properly. I'll admit that, when I was travelling around Burnley and the local towns, my name helped. My boss was Vic Halom, who played centre-forward for Sunderland when they beat Leeds in the 1973 FA Cup final, and was later at Oldham when I was coaching."

"I did three years with the company, New Earth Water Services, and I enjoyed my time with them. Then Jimmy sold up to a South African concern and, as often happens in those circumstances, they made some redundancies. I was coming up to sixty and so I thought it was time to take early retirement."

However, anyone who thought that Andy Lochhead was headed for a life of sitting by the fireside, reminiscing about his playing career, was mistaken. "I noticed that a lot of clubs were using ex-players as matchday hospitality hosts. Burnley didn't do anything like that and I knew from watching football around the country that there was a good source of revenue if clubs did it properly. In 2000 I approached Barry Colbie, who was then the chairman of Burnley, and asked him if I could do the job at Turf Moor. He agreed, and it works well to this day. There's me, Willie Irvine, who played for Burnley in the seventies, and Tommy Cummings, who was part of the side that won the league, then managed Villa for a spell just before I arrived. It's going well – we look after the sponsors, talk to them, slip in a few stories about when we were playing, sign autographs and have a few photos taken. The club does alright out of it, the guests are glad to meet us and everyone's happy."

Indeed, this avenue of work could have been a lucrative sideline for someone as well-loved as Andy Lochhead, had he chose to utilise his talents to the full. "My wife says I should have gone into after-dinner speaking, but it isn't really me. The money those lads get though; sometimes when we have a function at Turf Moor I hand over the cheque to the main speaker and it's incredible. There was one guy, who I won't name, came here a couple of years ago. He was delayed on the way over, spoke for 28 minutes, then left more or less straight afterwards. He'd been in the building less than an hour and on his way out I handed him a cheque for £3,000. I do some question and answer forums locally, and when Burnley are playing away I've done a couple at wherever they've been playing. I also write a column for the *Burnley Evening Telegraph*, but that's all."

Lochhead does, however, keep an eye on his former clubs, and although his heart will always be at Turf Moor, Villa remain firmly attached to his affections. Speaking after the club's defeat to Burnley in the 2004-05 Carling Cup, Lochhead's disappointment was evident. "They were very disappointing. I thought they'd be better than they were, but they didn't show much. Fair play to Doug Ellis, though. He came into the sponsors lounge after the match and said a few words. He was very gracious about it, and there's a few chairmen who wouldn't have been so obliging after a performance like that."

Of Gary Cahill, the promising central defender who Villa loaned to Burnley for much of the 2004-05 season, Lochhead is also full of praise. "A good 'un," is his measured opinion. "He hasn't put a foot wrong yet. He'll make it." The veteran centre-forward, who played against some of the best defenders the game has ever seen, couldn't help but make one last remark about the youngster, though. "I'd have straightened him out. I always was a touch player."

And warming to his theme, Lochhead gave a lament familiar to all of us who have long despaired of the way the game is increasingly being packaged as a non-contact sport. "In all my career I was only sent off once, for Burnley reserves against Bury reserves, and I didn't deserve that. But I wouldn't last two minutes these days. It was a man's game then, I can remember when Dick Edwards was centre-half for the Villa and I broke his nose when we collided going for the ball. I said 'sorry', he shrugged it off and we carried on."

Lochhead and his wife also make a point of watching Villa's games whenever they play in the north-west, work commitments permitting. "I like to see them do well," he says. "Especially when they play Blackburn," chipped in Mrs Lochhead. Old habits die hard.

Sammy Morgan

I met up with Sammy Morgan at Ipswich's spacious training ground on the edge of the town. Villa had drawn 1-1 at Fulham the previous night in a game chiefly memorable for two penalties missed by Juan Pablo Angel: "You wouldn't dare do that when Ron Saunders was manager," reflected Morgan.

Born in Belfast, in 1946, Sammy moved with his family to Great Yarmouth at the age of twelve. After leaving school he began work, first with a firm of accountants, and then attended teachers' training college at Clifton, Nottingham from 1968-71. Playing football for his local side Gorleston, of the Anglian Combination, he attracted the attention of Norwich City, then managed by Ron Saunders. However, Saunders decided not to pursue an interest in the young forward, and Morgan's then-manager, former Villa reserve player Roger Carter, recommended the player to former Villa Park colleague Gordon Lee, at the time manager of third division Port Vale.

Morgan made a big impression at Vale, particularly when scoring twice as his side came back from 1-4 down at home to draw with Aston Villa in a league match in March 1972. "Another few minutes and we'd have won," he now says. Morgan also made a big impression on the fans who watched him at Vale Park. "He was my first hero," says Ash Connor, a Vale follower for over thirty years and now a director of the Port Vale Supporters Trust. "At our level he was brilliant."

Morgan played 114 games for Vale, scoring 25 goals and doing well enough to impress the Villa manager Vic Crowe, who acted on the recommendation of Gordon Lee to snap up the Northern Irish centre-forward in the summer of 1973 for a fee of £20,000, plus £1,000 for every goal he scored for Villa during the following season. "Our chairman used to ring Doug Ellis every Saturday to ask if I'd scored," he remembers. It's not known whether Doug instructed the rest of the team not to pass to Sammy or allow him take any penalties.

Morgan played 44 times for Villa under Vic Crowe and his successor Ron Saunders, scoring 15 goals and winning praise for his whole-hearted approach to the game, which often got him into trouble with officialdom, most famously when playing for Villa in the 1974 FA Cup fourth round against Arsenal. Sent off for making two robust challenges on Arsenal keeper Bob Wilson in a 1-1 draw at Highbury, Morgan scored in Villa's victory in the replay, his punishment for dismissal later being rescinded. Chico Hamilton, though, remembers that although Sammy might have been a handful for opposition defences, he could also cause problems for his team-mates. "Many's the time we'd get to Bodymoor for training, only to find that Sammy had lost his contact lenses so we'd all be on the floor on our knees, looking for them. I swear he never learnt to put them in properly."

By now Morgan was a regular in the Northern Ireland team, during which time he realised that he had a famous former schoolmate. "I was from the Castlereagh estate in Belfast, George Best was from the Cregagh estate next to us. I'd got an old school photo, and it was only when I joined the Northern Ireland squad that I realised George had been at the same school, Nettlefield." Morgan played 18 times for Northern Ireland, scoring on three occasions, although such a modest record was hampered by the fact that the political situation meant the team were unable to play home games for much of his international career. Ulsterman Ernie Cunningham says of Sammy, "His most memorable performance was when he went face to face with England's Roy McFarland and the tackle resulted in the England central defender being badly injured. I believe McFarland did not play another international until late the following year and only added a few more caps to his collection."

Morgan's time at Villa began to draw to an end with the arrival of Ron Saunders in the summer of 1974. "I played a few games during the promotion season, but I had a serious groin injury so I missed the League Cup final. Keith Leonard took my place, and he stayed in the team when we got promoted. I played in the first game against Antwerp, but Ron put John Robson, who was a midfielder, in the number nine shirt for the second leg, even though the Belgians said they didn't fancy playing against me again. If I'm being honest, the first division was a bit of a big step up, but Ron broke the club's transfer record when he signed Andy Gray to take my place, and he wasn't a bad player."

Morgan moved to Brighton & Hove Albion, then in the third division, just before Christmas 1975, for a fee of £14,000. The manager at Brighton was none other than Peter Taylor, right-hand man to Brian Clough throughout the legendary manager's greatest moments. Clough had managed Brighton for a time following his rancorous departure from Derby but soon moved on for what would be an infamous 44-day tenure at Leeds United. Taylor had stayed with the south coast club, and Sammy says of the time, "Peter was a decent manager, but there was definitely something missing when he wasn't Brian's assistant. Neither of them was particularly successful on their own, but together they were unbeatable."

Taylor's acquisition of the centre-forward was no sudden fancy, as Sammy explains. "When I was at Vale, Cloughie and Peter had tried to take me to Derby on loan, but Gordon Lee turned them down. Peter must have remembered me from that time, and when Ron Saunders made me available I was off to Brighton."

Morgan's time at the Goldstone Ground started well enough, but was eventually to suffer a double blow. "Peter left to become assistant to Brian again, at Forest, and Alan Mullery took his place. Then Paul Futcher caught me in the face during a pre-season friendly with Luton and I broke a cheekbone. I was out for a few months, and when I returned I wasn't sure of my first team place. Alan would mix us round – there were three forwards, Ian Mellor, Peter Ward and myself, and I tended to be used in the away matches, when things were getting a bit tough. We got promoted to the second division in 1976-77, but I wanted regular first-team football so I asked for a transfer."

After 35 games and eight goals for Brighton, a fee of £15,000 saw Sammy move back into the third division, to Cambridge United, whose manager was another former Villa player and contemporary of Messrs Lee and Carter, Ron Atkinson. As you'd expect, Sammy still has vivid recollections of his time spent under the Atkinson management. "Ron always says that I was the biggest gamble of his career, because Cambridge had no money when he signed me." The gamble paid off, though, as Cambridge won promotion in the last game of the season. "We were playing Exeter. I'd been out injured but I was named as sub. They'd given me so many injections I couldn't feel my foot, but we were losing and needed to do something drastic. I came on and I still remember the *Cambridge Evening News* report saying that straightaway I hit the Exeter keeper so hard he could see the allotments that were behind the ground. I didn't score, but I was of more than enough nuisance value. We won 2-1 and got promoted."

By this time, Atkinson had left, the Hawthorns being the next stage of a managerial odyssey that created one of the most controversial and best-loved characters the game has ever seen. Morgan certainly remembers with fondness the brief period he spent under Big Ron's tutelage. "He had a simple philosophy – 'get forward'. He loved football; all that nonsense about the jewellery and the big time stuff, it was just an act. Deep down he was purely a football man, and he knew how he wanted it played. He could have a go at you if he thought you'd played badly, you'd have a go back at him and the next day it was forgotten. He hasn't changed, either. When he was manager at Villa I went up there with Norwich. He was at the ground, wearing a bathrobe and looking as though he'd just stepped from under a sun lamp. Next thing he's making us both a cup of tea and chatting away about when we were at Cambridge together."

The arrival of John Doherty saw Morgan's departure grow imminent. "He made it clear that I wasn't in his thoughts," is the brief summing-up of Doherty's opinion, and the summer of 1978 saw Sammy off to the Netherlands, to play for Sparta Rotterdam after having scored four goals in 37 games for Cambridge.

For a country that had spent much of the past decade thrilling to the all-conquering Ajax side and then a national team that must rank as one of the best never to win a World Cup, the sight of the raw-boned Morgan was somewhat of a culture shock. But whatever their preconceptions, football supporters the world over appreciate a player who will give everything in the service of the club they follow. Morgan enthuses about his time in the Netherlands, having clearly enjoyed himself. "We got a good result against Ajax, then in my third game I got the winner against Feyenoord in their local derby. Sparta had a good tradition, but had fallen on hard times – a bit like Villa when I was first there. The supporters liked the way I played, and I was popular with them."

Morgan also made the acquaintance while playing in Rotterdam of a man who would go on to become one of the world's greatest coaches. "Louis van Gaal was in the team with me. He was a midfielder, and although he wasn't an outstanding player, he was a great technician and a very serious student of the game. There were some good sides around at the time, not up to the level of a few years earlier when Feyenoord and Ajax had both won the European Cup, but the Van der Kerkhof brothers and Rudi Krol were still playing. It was a totally different style to playing in England, though. Someone once said 'In England, football is for the fans. In Italy, it's for the players. In Holland, it's for the coaches.' That was true when I was there. Total football was the prerogative of the national team, but the domestic game was like chess. I did well there because I was a bit different from what they were used to."

Morgan had a season with Sparta and then transferred to Groningen, helping them to promotion to the top ERE division of the Dutch league, before retiring in 1980. He then returned to East Anglia and his first love, playing part-time for Gorleston, who had then joined the Eastern Counties league, and becoming a teacher in Great Yarmouth. "I taught maths and PE for seventeen years from 1980. I loved it at first, then I realised that the kids didn't have the same enthusiasm as I had, so I started thinking about doing something different.

"I'd been involved in football since going back to teaching and had been coaching with Norwich's youth set-up for ten years, when the job of Academy Director came up in 1997, and I was there until the summer of 2004. I was proud of my achievement there, and I was disappointed when they chose not to renew my contract." Some of the players who Morgan had helped within the development programme included Darren Eadie, Ade Akinbiyi, Craig Bellamy, Chris Sutton and Robert Green, so it was no surprise that he found himself with a job offer soon afterwards, and one which did not involve much of a change of circumstance.

"An opportunity came up at Ipswich. We'd always got on well despite being big rivals, and the director of their academy, Bryan Klug, asked me to fill the vacancy they had for a Head of Education.

I take care of the education programme for the players age 16 and over, monitor the progress of the schoolboys on our books, do some scouting and coach the younger lads. I like the set-up and I'm happy here."

At the time of our meeting, Villa were due at Portman Road for an FA Youth cup-tie, and Morgan was naturally interested in the set-up of his opponents' Academy and, in particular, the progress of his countryman Steve Davis. "A tremendous prospect" was the Morgan verdict, although he could be accused of having mixed feelings on the subject. The Morgan family, his wife Alison and their son and daughter, remain staunch Villa supporters while Sammy himself harbours warm feelings for the club. "I was extremely privileged to play for Aston Villa. They're a great club and they always make me very welcome whenever I return."

Also available from Heroes Publishing

McMULLAN TO O'LEARY

Claret and Blue Managers

McMullan to O'Leary is an account of the 20 men who have enjoyed (or should that be endured?) time in the managerial hot-seat at Villa Park. Find out: Which Villa manager was accused of being a war-time collaborator; Who kept a resignation letter in his desk ready to be signed throughout his time at Villa Park; What Big Ron really thought of Deadly Doug; The reason behind John Gregory's shock departure – by the man who knows him best; And David O'Leary's hopes for the future.

Contains exclusive interviews with Villa managers: Tommy Cummings, Tommy Docherty, Graham Turner, Graham Taylor, Josef Venglos, Ron Atkinson, Brian Little and David O'Leary.

Also includes the reminiscences of players including: Dennis Mortimer, Gary Shaw, Tony Morley, Allan Evans, Dennis Jackson, Harry Burrows, Alan Deakin, Brian Godfrey, Jim Cumbes, Chris Nicholl, Steve McMahon, Paul Birch and Ian Olney.
And, the unique insights of former Villa chairman Sir William Dugdale and Rosina Barton, the widow of Villa's European Cup winning manager.

232pp - Price £8.99
ISBN: 0-9543884-1-0

Also available from Heroes Publishing

CHAMPIONS
1980/81 Revisited

Following on from another round of bloody boardroom battles, against the backdrop of some of the best players in the club's post-War history leaving, in the face of a doubting and dismissive media, and with a young and inexperienced squad, fourteen players wrote themselves into Villa legend. At long last, a new generation of fans could feel what their ancestors took for granted. Aston Villa, after a 71-year wait, were Champions once more.

A full, month-by-month guide to Villa's 1980/81 campaign with the Foreword by European Cup-winning striker, and Villa fan, Gary Shaw. Champions includes exclusive interviews with the players who returned the club to the pinnacle of the sport, along with the memories of supporters and those who captured the Class of '81 in print and through the camera lens.

232pp - Price £8.99
ISBN: 0-9543884-2-9

Heroes Publishing is always on the look out for talented writers.
Samples to: PO Box 1703, Perry Barr, Birmingham, B42 1UZ
or see our website at: www.heroespublishing.com